On the Trail of the Poets of the
Great War

EDMUND BLUNDEN

Other guides in the Battleground Europe Series:

Walking the Salient *by* Paul Reed
Ypres - Sanctuary Wood and Hooge *by* Nigel Cave
Ypres - Hill 60 *by* Nigel Cave
Ypres - Messines Ridge *by* Peter Oldham
Ypres - Polygon Wood *by* Nigel Cave

Walking the Somme *by* Paul Reed
Somme - Gommecourt *by* Nigel Cave
Somme - Serre *by* Jack Horsfall & Nigel Cave
Somme - Beaumont Hamel *by* Nigel Cave
Somme - Thiepval *by* Michael Stedman
Somme - La Boisselle *by* Michael Stedman
Somme - Fricourt *by* Michael Stedman
Somme - Carnoy-Montauban *by* Graham Maddocks
Somme - Pozieres *by* Graham Keech
Somme - Courcelette *by* Paul Reed
Somme - Boom Ravine *by* Trevor Pidgeon

Arras - Vimy Ridge *by* Nigel Cave
Arras - Bullecourt *by* Graham Keech

Hindenburg Line *by* Peter Oldham
Epehy *by* Bill Mitchinson
Riqueval *by* Bill Mitchinson

Boer War - The Relief of Ladysmith, Colenso, Spion Kop *by* Lewis Childs
Boer War - The Siege of Ladysmith *by* Lewis Childs

Accrington Pals Trail *by* WilliamTurner

On the Trail of The Poets of The Great War: Wilfred Owen
by Helen McPhail and Philip Guest

Gallipoli *by* Nigel Steel

Battleground Europe Series guides in preparation:

La Basseé - Givenchy *by* Michael Orr
La Basseé - Neuve Chapelle 1915 *by* Geoff Bridger
Walking Arras *by* Paul Reed
Arras - Monchy le Preux *by* Colin Fox
Somme - Following the Ancre *by* Michael Stedman
Somme - High Wood *by* Terry Carter
Somme - Advance to Victory 1918 *by* Michael Stedman
Somme - Ginchy *by* Michael Stedman
Somme - Combles *by* Paul Reed
Somme - Beaucourt *by* Michael Renshaw

Walking Verdun *by* Paul Reed

Isandhlwana *by* Ian Knight and Ian Castle
Rorkes Drift *by* Ian Knight and Ian Castle

With the continued expansion of the Battleground series a Battleground Europe Club has been formed to benefit the reader. The purpose of the Club is to keep members informed of new titles and key developments by way of a quarterly newsletter, and to offer many other reader-benefits. Membership is free and by registering an interest you can help us predict print runs and thus maintain prices at their present levels. Please call the office 01226 734555, or send your name and address along with a request for more information to:

Battleground Europe Club
Pen & Sword Books Ltd, 47 Church Street, Barnsley, South Yorkshire S70 2AS

On the Trail of the Poets of the Great War

EDMUND BLUNDEN

Helen McPhail
and
Philip Guest

Series editor
Nigel Cave

LEO COOPER

First published in 1999 by
LEO COOPER
an imprint of
Pen & Sword Books Limited
47 Church Street, Barnsley, South Yorkshire S70 2AS

ISBN 0 85052 678 7

A CIP catalogue of this book is available
from the British Library

Printed by Redwood Books Limited
Trowbridge, Wiltshire

*For up-to-date information on other titles produced under the Leo Cooper imprint,
please telephone or write to:*
Pen & Sword Books Ltd, FREEPOST, 47 Church Street
Barnsley, South Yorkshire S70 2AS
Telephone 01226 734222

CONTENTS

Christ's Hospital Quadrangle, Horsham (the new site, built to house the school when it moved from the City of London in 1902): Big School in the centre, class rooms on either side.

SERIES EDITOR'S INTRODUCTION

One of the joys of being the commissioning editor in this series of books is that I get quite a wide discretion on the topics and areas covered. I felt that there was space for books on individuals who had written extensively of their experiences in the war, and amongst the best known of these are the war poets. Although I must confess some ambivalence over the writings of Wilfred Owen, it is undoubtedly true that he wrote with searing power, he is a highly 'popular' poet, and seemed an ideal candidate with which to start. An author sprang instantly to mind, knowing as I did of Helen McPhail's senior position in the Wilfred Owen Association. Philip Guest - surely one of the most congenial of battlefield tour companions? - was almost as enthusiastic about Owen and has a detailed knowledge of the battlefields. The combination was set up, and the first of the books on the Trail of the Poets of the Great War series came into being.

This, the second book in the series, came about as the result of a casual conversation when I was giving a talk to the Surrey branch of the WFA. A member mentioned that Claire Blunden, Edmund's widow, had been on a recent battlefield tour. Wonderful coincidence! For when I first became interested in the Great War some thirty or more years ago, *Undertones of War* was one of the first books I read after the classics of the Royal Welch Fusiliers group - Sassoon, Graves and Richards. I considered - and still do - that *Undertones* was probably one of the three or four books that I would keep should the time ever come to give up my Great War collection of books. Another would be Bernard Adams's rather unknown, but beautiful, *Nothing of Importance* - another of the RWF 'school'.

The reason for my enthusiasm lay in the fact that due to the personal contacts of Helen and Philip with Claire Blunden they were able to have unrivalled access to papers, photographs and books belonging to Edmund Blunden himself. For Claire Blunden's co-operation and support of this project I am enormously grateful, as I know the writers are also.

When I first mentioned Blunden as a possibility for the series - and before the existence of this treasure-trove had been revealed - several people to whom I mentioned the idea felt that he was not sufficiently well known to justify such coverage. But the opportunity of the extra material, combined with my enormous respect for the author, was sufficient to carry the publishers, and I hope that this book will go a long way to reminding people of the existence of this brilliant prose writer, as well as his merit as a 'war' poet.

Helen and Philip have done a superb job with this book; it is not an easy form of guide to write, a delicate balance between events, the individual's roles and actions, literary criticism and placing actions 'then' on to the contemporary ground of France and Flanders. It has been a real pleasure to edit this book and I think it has enhanced considerably the study of Blunden's literary works. It also places Edmund Blunden's Great War writing in the context of his life, which in his case was a long and fascinating one, giving the book an extra dimension and balance.

Edmund Blunden's writings on the Great War are of great sublety, and perhaps this has detracted from a wider popularity - the angrier (or, rather, more overtly angry) writings of Owen, Sasson and Graves possibly require a less detailed understanding of the Great War as it struck individuals in order to be able to understand their vigorous message. I am sure that this book will be of significant assistance in understanding more fully the works of a great author.

Nigel Cave
Ely Place, London

SELECT CHRONOLOGY

1896	1 November	Born, London
1900		Family moves to Yalding, Kent
1909		Enters Christ's Hospital, Horsham
1914		Wins scholarship (Classics) to Oxford
	October	First publication of poems
1915	August	Volunteers. Commissioned in 10th Btn Royal Sussex Regiment
1916	Spring	Joins 11th Royal Sussex in France Summer: active service at Festubert, Cuinchy and Givenchy
	August	Battalion moves to the Somme
	Sept-Nov	In action in the Ancre valley and at Thiepval
	November	Battalion moves to the Ypres Salient
1917	January	Award of Military Cross gazetted
	31 July	In the battalion attack at St. Julien,Third Ypres (`Passchendaele')
1918	January	Battalion moves to the Somme area
	February	Returns from Gouzeaucourt to training camp in England
	June	Marries Mary Daines (two daughters, one son, marriage dissolved 1931)
1919	17 February	Demobbed
	August	Death of daughter Joy, aged five weeks
	October	Takes up place at Oxford
1920		Leaves Oxford for *The Athenaeum*
1922	April	Receives the Hawthornden Prize for Poetry
1924		Professor of English Literature, Imperial University of Tokyo
1927		Returns to England, to *The Nation*
1928	November	Publication of *Undertones of War*
1930	November	Publication of *De Bello Germanico*, a fragment of trench history written in 1918
1931	February	Appointed Fellow and Tutor in English, Merton College, Oxford
1933		Marries Sylva Norman (marriage dissolved 1945)
1940		Serves with Oxford University O.T.C. as map instructor

1945		Joins *The Times Literary Supplement*
1945	May	Marries Claire Poynting (four daughters)
1947		Returns to Japan as Cultural Liaison Officer with the British Mission
1950		Returns to *The Times Literary Supplement*
1951		Created CBE
1953		Becomes Professor of English, University of Hong Kong. Visits Japan on lecture tours
1956		Awarded Queen's Gold Medal for Poetry
1962		Created Companion of Literature
1964		Leaves Hong Kong, settles in Long Melford, Suffolk
1966	February	Elected Professor of Poetry, Oxford
1968		Resigns on medical advice
1974	20 January	Dies at Long Melford

Publications

Poems 1913 and 1914; *Poems Translated from the French* (1914); *The Harbingers* (May 1916); *Pastorals* (June 1916); *The Waggoner* (August 1920); *Poems Chiefly from Manuscript* by John Clare (ed. Blunden and Porter, 1920); *The Shepherd and Other Poems of Peace and War* (1922); *The Bonaventure* (journal of a voyage to South America, 1922); *Christ's Hospital: a Retrospect* (1923); *A Song to David* by Christopher Smart (ed. Blunden), 1924; *Masks of Time* (June 1925); *Shelley and Keats: As they struck their Contemporaries* (ed. Blunden, 1925); *English Poems* (June 1925); *On the Poems of Henry Vaughan* (March 1927); *Retreat* (May 1928); *Leigh Hunt's Examiner Examined* (July 1928); *Japanese Garland* (September 1928); *The Autobiography of Leigh Hunt* (ed. Blunden, September 1928); *Undertones of War,* November 1928); *The Poems of William Collins* (ed. Blunden, June 1929); *Nature in English Literature* (1929); *Near and Far* (September 1929); *Leigh Hunt* (biography, May 1930); *De Bello Germanico* (November 1930); *The Poems 1914-1930* (December 1930); *Sketches in the Life of John Clare* and *The Poems of Wilfred Owen* (March 1931); *Votive Tables: Studies Chiefly Appreciative of English Authors and Books* (November 1931); *The Face of England* (March 1932); *A Halfway House* (November 1932); *Charles Lamb and his Contemporaries* (1933); *We'll Shift Our Ground* (novel, by Blunden and Sylva Norman, January 1933); *The Mind's Eye* (April 1934); *Choice or Chance* (November 1934); *An Elegy and Other Poems* (November 1937); *Poems 1930-1940* (January 1941); *English Villages* (September 1941); *Thomas Hardy* (in `English Men of Letters' series, February 1943); *Cricket Country* (April 1944); *Shells by a Stream* (October 1944); *Shelley* (biography, April 1946); *After the Bombing* (October 1949); John Keats (in `Writers and their Works', September 1950); *Poems by Ivor Gurney* (September 1954); *Charles Lamb* (in `Writers and their Works', November 1954); *Poems of Many Years* (June 1957); *War Poets 1914-1918* (`Writers and their Works' series, July 1958); *A Hong Kong House* (September 1962); *Eleven Poems* (1966); *The Midnight Skaters: Poems for Young Readers* (1968).

INTRODUCTION

Edmund Blunden in 1917 or 1918, wearing his Military Cross medal

Edmund Blunden occupies a unique position in relation to the First World War; his classic memoir *Undertones of War* unites readers of otherwise widely separated attitudes to life and war. For those with little interest in military history, his humane warmth, close observation of man and nature and delicate precision of language are illuminating and persuasive - while the subtle but clear descriptions of Flanders and the Somme, of life in the trenches, the appreciation of life and friendship that shine through, are a revelation for readers who are not generally drawn to poets.

Because this book is largely concerned with Blunden's rich variety of experiences between 1916 and 1918, *Undertones of War* has been our inevitable and valuable point of reference - and a continual temptation to give lengthy quotations on almost every page; there are indeed extracts from it, both prose and poetry, but we have used it as our source-book alongside the usual range of military memoirs, diaries, biographies, etc., and other poems by Blunden.

For those who wish to follow Blunden in his own words, references are given in this text in square brackets, with the indication U/W and the page number in the Penguin Modern Classics edition. Blunden's war took him to many well-known locations, and by following the indications in *Undertones of War* it is possible to follow him with great accuracy and sympathy.

The circumstances of writing *Undertones* are worth noting. Blunden's first venture into print with images of war came with *The Shepherd and Other Poems of Peace and War,* but the full and considered prose record of his experiences had to wait for several years after the Armistice. In 1918 he sketched out a fragment of description of life in the trenches but this was not published until many years later, under the title of *De Bello Germanico.* It was in the late 1920s, when Blunden was in Japan, that he wrote his war memoirs, with very little in the way of diary or maps - and no veterans to talk it over with. The accuracy of his memory is astonishing, and perhaps shows how deeply the whole experience had marked him: the individuals spring to life off the page, the lyrical descriptions of wild life surviving behind and between the trenches indicate how he clung to natural elements in the unnatural surroundings of war, the quiet ironies show fellow-feeling with the young officer he had been ten years earlier.

There are occasional inaccuracies of date or sequence in the incidents – although, checking against battalion diaries, it is remarkable to see how few they are; but there is no doubting the full truth of what he observed and how it remained in his thoughts and his spirit.

ACKNOWLEDGEMENTS

In a note dated November 1964 Edmund Blunden commented that in 'this miscellany' (i.e. *Undertones of War*) he has made little mention of some of the places and battle zones known to the 11th Royal Sussex; his album contains no postcards or photographs of the River Ancre, for example, or the area round Gouzeaucourt. Equally, the album shows more places than people; tantalisingly, he raises the possibility of a supplementary volume, which was never written - and, as he points out, cameras were forbidden at the front, and 'very few succeeded in breaking the rule'. We are all the more grateful for his clear-eyed and humane descriptions of his comrades in arms.

In presenting this interpretation of *Undertones of War* and various poems, with many images from Blunden's private album, our first and deepest debt of gratitude goes to Claire Blunden, for her interest, help and generosity. Her practical, discreet and sympathetic support has made the preparation and writing of the book an enjoyable exploration of one man's war and his writing; without her the personal tone of the memoirs and poems could not have been illustrated from the carefully assembled and annotated personal collection.

Warm thanks are due to Piet Chielens, of Ypres, and to Christ's Hospital for information and permission to illustrate Blunden's links with his much-loved school. We are also grateful for the following permissions:

Robyn Marsack, for the chronology, p.8-9;

the IWM, for the following pictures: 28,29, 36, 67, 72, 73, 76, 77, 78, 89, 102/3, 116, 138-9

Christ's Hospital, page 5, 15, 20

Country Life, for the pictures of Christ's Hospital, p.16

Professor J.E.Morpurgo for permission to reprint part of a letter to Hector Buck, p.130-1

Natwest Group Archives, p.65

Tom Donovan Publishing for the photograph by Peter T. Scott, page 95

Crown copyright material in the Public Record Office is reproduced by permission of the Controller of Her Majesty's Stationery Office, p.96

The prose and poetry extracts from *Undertones of War* are reprinted by permission of the Peters Fraser & Dunlop Group Ltd.

Chapter One

'BUT CRICKET'S NOT EVERYTHING'

(Charles Blunden, in a letter to his son Edmund, aged 8)

Edmund Blunden lived for more than half a century after the 1918 Armistice, for he was still a schoolboy in 1914, and passed through the dangers of war without even the slightest physical wound. He did not escape unaffected however, and for the rest of his long life - like so many other survivors - he was haunted by what he had lived through.

The young officer who was posted to the 11th Battalion, the Royal Sussex Regiment in May 1915 was small, neat, bright-eyed and observant. Friends described him as 'bird-like', and his restless activity and trim physique bear out this impression.

Like the great majority of officer volunteers in the First World War, Edmund Blunden came from a public school: but his was an unusual school, he was an unusual young officer, and his education was perhaps the single most important influence in his life. The eldest son of the headmaster of a small grammar school and his teacher wife, (Charles and Margaret, known to their children as 'Pugg' and 'Mugg'), Edmund was born on 1 November 1896 in London but spent the happy

Line drawing of Yalding Church.

formative years of his childhood in Yalding, Kent. His parents moved here in 1900, and its surroundings, the microcosm of humanity represented in a busy farming village at the end of the Victorian era, became the perfect setting for a bright, observant and sociable boy who was intensely sensitive to his rural surroundings. It was in Yalding that he discovered the fears and delights of water in the landscape – mill-ponds, fishing, streams and flood meadows - and also what became another abiding love, cricket.

These themes – human nature and friendship, the beauties and threats of nature, the delights of cricket - run through his writing and sustained him through everything.

By the time Edmund was eleven he was clearly outstripping his

Cleaves School house, Yalding.

contemporaries in terms of intellect and, eager and intellectually curious, he needed a more challenging educational atmosphere. No funds were available for a conventional public-school education, but a very distinctive school was available which might have been designed expressly to bring the best out of this enthusiastic, energetic and sensitive boy.

Christ's Hospital was a very ancient foundation which in 1902 moved from its original site in the City of London to extensive new premises near Horsham. The education it offered was conventional in content, based on the glories of the classics and of English literature, with a strong element of sport, but the setting and ethos that it offered were - and remain - unique. Its primary criteria for taking in a boy or girl are that the prospective pupil should be suitably deserving in personal as well as intellectual terms; the family's capacity to pay the fees is not relevant to the selection of pupils, and many benefit from free places.

Pupils still wear the traditional heavy buttoned gown and yellow stockings, and many distinguished names appear in the school records. It hardly seems too strong an expression to say that Edmund Blunden fell in love with the school, absorbing its intellectual offerings greedily but also finding its humanely moral and personal approach fully in sympathy with his own instincts. More even than this, the school provided him with an intellectual ancestry: Old Blues, as former pupils are known, include many very famous names in English literature, and as the young Edmund Blunden began to explore poetry, both to read and to write, he was proud to share the literary heritage of Charles

Presentation issued _____ 7 - JUL 1909 _____, in consequence of the boy named herein having been successful in a Competitive Examination of Candidates from **ENDOWED SCHOOLS.**

To the Right Honourable, Right Worshipful, and Worshipful the Almoners of CHRIST'S HOSPITAL, LONDON.

The humble Petition of _Chas. Edmund Blunden_

of the Parish of _Yalding, Maidstone, Kent_

SHEWETH

THAT THE PETITIONER is in need of assistance towards the maintenance and education of his children, as evidenced by the answers to interrogatories on the other side, and he beseeches your Worships, in your usual Charity to Widows, Orphans, and Families, who stand in need of Relief, to grant the ADMISSION into CHRIST'S HOSPITAL, of

BORN, 1st Nov.r 1896

Edmund Charles Blunden

son of _Chas. E. Blunden_ and _Georgina Margaret Blunden_

his wife, there to be Educated and Maintained among other poor Children; and instructed in the Christian Religion, according to the principles, doctrine, and discipline of the Church of England;* and the Petitioner hereby consents and agrees to leave the said Child, if admitted, entirely under the control of the Authorities of the said Hospital during the time that he shall remain therein, and promises to discharge the Hospital of the said Child whensoever the Council of Almoners shall require the same.†

N.— 14 SEP 1909

Petitioner's Signature and Address.
Chas. E. Blunden
Congelow, Yalding, Maidstone

* Any Petitioner desiring to avail himself of the special exemption from Religious Services and Instruction provided by Clause 80 of the Scheme must give written notice thereof at the time of lodging this Petition at the Office of the Foundation.
† Unless the Council of Almoners are satisfied of the responsibility of the Petitioner, a Bond may be required of some responsible person to secure the ultimate discharge of the Child.

ENT.º REGISTER FOL 289.

§ This statement may be signed by a Justice of the Peace resident in the Parish, instead of by the Minister and Churchwardens. In either case the signatures of 3 Householders must be procured.

WE, the Minister, Churchwardens, and others of the Parish of _Yalding_ in the County of _Kent_ whose Names are hereunto subscribed, do Certify, That we have perused the foregoing Petition and the answers to Interrogatories on page 2 hereof filled up by the Petitioner, and to the best of our knowledge and belief consider them to be true and correct.

Witness our Hands this 16th day of _July_ 19 0 9

John Rowland Leigh Minister. { If the Father be Minister, the Clergyman of an adjoining parish is to sign here.

Robert Norton
Charles E Fletcher } Churchwardens.

Frank Bush
J. Rewn
Samuel Williams } Three Householders in the above Parish.

ADMITTED EDUCATION COMMITTEE
& CLOTHED   15 SEP 1909

Christ's Hospital entrance award to Edmund Charles Blunden. CHRISTS HOSPITAL

Lamb, Leigh Hunt and Coleridge. This trio all acknowledged the strong impression of the school in their lives, in the late eighteenth century, and they in turn were felt as a benign influence on later generations. The unique requirements for entry encouraged three qualities which can be seen clearly throughout Blunden's life and which appear consciously in his correspondence and other writing: gratitude to the school (known as 'Housie' or 'Housey'), brotherhood between pupils, and a desire to do one's best, out of gratitude and pride in the school. The sense of true social equality encouraged a democratic brotherhood; this, combined with a teaching staff who were fully in sympathy with the foundation's principles, gave the pupils a keen sense of belonging and sharing which was as valuable as their intellectual achievements.

This privileged and distinctive education created something of a gap between Edmund and the rest of his family; although they were, and continued to be, a close-knit

Christ's Hospital: the arch from the old London buildings reconstructed at the Horsham site.

Dinner parade at Christ's Hospital.
COUNTRY LIFE

and loving household, when financial disasters struck the sensitive and intelligent eldest son was spared a certain amount of domestic distress and when he returned for the school holidays his horizons were broader than those of his siblings.

Perhaps his life at school was best summed up by one of his teachers, a young history master called 'Teddy' Edwards, who became a life-long friend. Forty-five years later he wrote of his young pupil:

Apparently here was the really perfect boy, keen as mustard in class and in games, who was eccentric in one respect only ... he wrote poems! I found him a nervous-speaking, weakly-built boy, bulging with brains and bursting with enthusiasm.

Writing poetry was an early and enduring passion for the young Blunden. He brought his enquiring eye and childhood delight in nature to his expanding knowledge of other languages and their structure, appreciating the tools through which he could express his observations and emotions. School slang was added gleefully to his life-long pleasure in old rural vocabulary; obscure names and references from old country crafts and pastimes would appear at unexpected moments, and in due course were a comfort in the bleak conditions of the Western Front. This growing facility with words was matched with physical elegance of expression, for Christ's Hospital laid great emphasis on calligraphy and Edmund took pains to develop a stylish and easily legible style of hand-writing. Determined to pursue literature, he persuaded the official school librarian to allow him a key to the school library, and thereafter explored it regularly and widely.

Edmund Blunden went to Christ's Hospital in 1909, at the age of 12. Early in 1913 *The Blue*, the school magazine, printed his first published poem, followed by several others in due course, all of them showing the characteristics of observation and description, dialect and rural tradition which would endure throughout his mature adult work. In 1914 Blunden was prepared to share his poetry with the wider world and paid for just over forty poems to be published, together with a similar number translated from French. In more orthodox areas of school work he was drawn to French as well as the classics, and to the Natural History Society (based on his childhood love of Yalding and the Kent countryside) for a deeper knowledge of plant and animal life. Finally, he became 'Senior Grecian', the Christ's Hospital term for head boy. Grecians were boys considered capable of winning an Oxford or Cambridge scholarship and who stayed at the school until they were 18 for this purpose. At this stage of their school career, their uniform incorporated a grander version of the standard coat, with

Sporting success at school.

fourteen large buttons and turned-up velvet cuffs. Winning one of these senior places usually brought with it an award from the school itself, so that successful pupils could continue to enjoy a free education until they left university.

Another of Blunden's great talents at school (and subsequently) was for making friends; he was a popular and attractive character, and Christ's Hospital provided some of his closest life-long friendships. From posterity's viewpoint, one of the most important of these was with Hector Buck, who quickly became and remained a close friend for sixty years. They corresponded regularly throughout all these years, and the publication of many of these letters reveals their mutually supportive relationship. Another important friendship that he valued during the war was with George Rheam, selected by Blunden as the beneficiary of his university scholarship should he fail to return from the war (see below).

Edmund Blunden was accustomed to wearing khaki by the time that the First World War broke out, for the Officers' Training Corps was a compulsory activity. He did not join the army immediately, however, but remained at Christ's Hospital until the end of the school year in July 1915, to complete his preparation for university. A month later he moved from the seniority of 'Senior Grecian', put aside his classical and literary concerns - and the Oxford scholarship which these had indeed earned him - and took his letters of recommendation for a commission to the Royal Sussex Regiment headquarters in Chichester.

Training followed, at Weymouth, Shoreham and Ireland. The Shoreham camp was near enough for Blunden to walk home, and quiet enough to give him time to pursue his life-long hobby of exploring bookshops - and also to write poetry, experimenting with longer poems than at school. It was in the spring of 1916 that he published three little collections of poems, the first dedicated to an 'Old Blue', Leigh Hunt, and the second to the tragic rural poet John Clare. He was concerned in his poetry to celebrate his surroundings, presenting finely-observed rural settings and individuals.

Soon after this, and still early in the spring of 1916, Blunden was sent back to Shoreham where, still wholly ignorant of the nature of the war that awaited him, the nineteen-year-old second lieutenant received his posting and left England for the first time in his life.

Edmund Blunden's England: home, school, army training, university and post-war life.

Bury St Edmunds
Cambridge
Long Melford
Oxford
LONDON
Horsham
Yalding
Christs' Hospital
Dover
Chichester
Shoreham
Weymouth

One of the poems that he wrote during the period between enlisting and leaving for France is called 'The Gods of the Earth Beneath': he speaks in the voice of the god of things that burrow and creep, with six brothers who are the gods of rooted plants, of rivers, of minerals and treasure hidden underground, of waters that vanish underground, of water lilies, and of river beds. This fanciful image enables him to describe at length the enduring strength of the natural world, the power of the earth's elements which will survive as long as the earth itself survives. Blunden's understanding of nature, its significance for him, is laid out with delight in the language of brook and hedgerow, pond and stream, trees, birds and flowers, as if he is defining his personal points of reference in the English countryside before he departs to the dangers of war.

Notes and Sources
More Than a Brother, Correspondence between Edmund Blunden and Hector Buck, 1917-1967, ed. Carol Z. Rothkopf and Barry Webb, Sexton Press, 1996
Edmund Blunden, Selected Poems, ed. Robyn Marsack, Carcanet, 1982

Chapter Two

'THE BROODING PRESENCE OF WAR'
[U/W, P.42]

Blunden's notebook for poetry in the trenches: left with his school-friend George Rheam while he was on leave, it was later presented to Christ's Hospital. CHRIST'S HOSPITAL

Edmund Blunden was lucky to survive the war untouched, for his war service took him to many of the places which had unwanted fame forced upon them by battles and circumstances.

Having taken his commission with the 10th Battalion Royal Sussex Regiment, he eventually joined the 11th (Service) Battalion (1st South Down). This was one of three battalions raised by Lieutenant-Colonel Lowther, M.P., in 1914; the other two, 12th and 13th, were known as the 2nd and 3rd South Down battalions. At Victoria Station for embarkation, accompanied by his mother, the young man - who, slight of build, certainly looked no more than his age of 19 - had a brief conversation about military matters with two experienced soldiers ('a lugubriously merry Highlander and a sturdy Engineer') returning to the B.E.F. One asked his age and, in response to the young officer's reply, echoed what must surely have been his mother's attitude: 'Only a boy - only a boy' [U/W, p.16]).

George Rheam. Blunden was still sufficiently close to his schooldays to be very conscious of those who remained in the classrooms of Christ's Hospital. Before leaving for France he addressed a sealed letter to the school Governors, to be opened in the event of his death. It expresses 'the foremost of my dying wishes', the wish that his school scholarship for classics (worth £70 p.a.) should be given to his friend George Rheam. Rheam, he stated, wished to become an electrical engineer after attending the City and Guilds Technology College, Finsbury, and would not be able to achieve this without financial support. As he stated at the end of the letter,

I long to see him doing well. This is why, Sirs, I ask that you be so good as to let my exhibition go to him: if he can by any means win through, I shall rest content. That is my dying wish.

Blunden and his draft crossed to Boulogne early in May 1916, and endured a brief training period at the notorious and dismal camp at Etaples, known to the troops as Eatapples, Eatables, or Heeltaps. Two incidents marked his stay there, neither of them encouraging: the theft of his ebony walking stick, which had once belonged to his grandfather, and a narrow escape from death when a defective grenade burst during instruction. It killed the Sergeant-Major who was giving the demonstration together with several officers standing nearby.

Orders soon came to join the battalion, holding the line near Festubert. It was early in May when he took the train via Béthune to Locon, to the Brigade office; orders here were to report to his unit at Le Touret, not far from Béthune, where he joined it in the evening of 14 May 1916. Blunden's war had begun.

The battalion was holding the line on the British front north of La Bassée canal, just south of Neuve Chapelle and not far from Festubert.

Letter to be sent to the school Governors in the event of his death, recommending that they award his scholarship to George Rheam for his further education.

To the Governors of Christ's Hospital.

Sirs,

By the time that this letter is put before you, my death in action will have been noticed. I ask you therefore, Sirs, particularly to consider what is the foremost of my dying wishes.

In July 1915 you were so generous as to award me (then Senior Grecian of Christ's Hospital) an Exhibition for classics to the value of £70 p. a. This will now pass from me; but I wonder whether you would do me the great last honour of giving the exhibition, or part of it, to my friend George Turner Jatham Rheam of Coleridge A, Christ's Hospital. He is hoping to become an electrical engineer, and first of all to enter the City and Guilds Technical College, Finsbury; this ideal he cannot realise without help, and I long to see him doing well. This is why, Sirs, I ask that you be so good as to let my exhibition go to him : if he can by any means win through, I shall rest content.

That is my dying wish.

I am,
Sirs,
Your obedient Servant,
Edmund Charles Blunden,
2nd Lt.

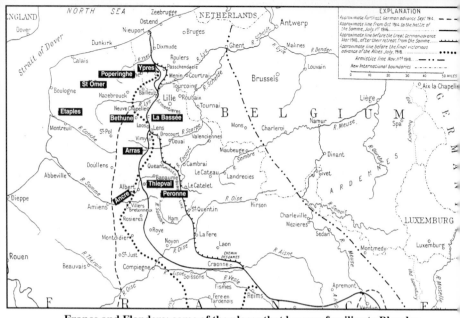

France and Flanders: some of the places that became familiar to Blunden, 1916-1918.

The war had been active here from its early days, with fighting around La Bassée, Festubert and Givenchy (with the Indian Corps playing a prominent part), followed by Givenchy and Cuinchy in January and February 1915. The battle of Neuve Chapelle came a month later, with attacks on Aubers in May 1915.

A few days later there was fighting at Festubert, again involving the Indian Corps. Divisions from England and Canada also attacked the German front line, and succeeded in advancing about 1000 yards. The 1st Battalion Royal Welch Fusiliers were in action on the same day, 15 May, and it was a group of men from this battalion which captured Canadian Orchard (where Blunden would be in the front line a year later), under the command of Captain Stockwell. Their advance was not held, although units of the 1st Canadian Division recaptured the orchard a few days later. The 1st Royal Welch lost nearly three-quarters of its strength and command of the survivors fell to Stockwell.

Stockwell was a professional soldier in every sense. Later, holding the rank of Lieutenant-Colonel, he commanded the 1st Royal Welch Fusiliers on the Somme at Bois Français (close to Fricourt, Mametz and Carnoy) where Siegfried Sassoon and Robert Graves were with the battalion. Stockwell, depicted in Sassoon's *Memoirs of an Infantry Officer* as Kinjack, was known to his men (and to Graves and Sassoon) as 'Buffalo Bill', an indication of his character as a soldier.

BÉTHUNE – Le Befroi et la Cathédrale

We of course had known and at once enjoyed Béthune before any considerable destruction befell (summer, 1916)

Blunden's personal album, two views of Béthune, pictured in 1918.

There was more fighting around Givenchy in June 1915 (IV Corps). Not far away, the Battle of Loos began in September with subsidiary action farther north of Loos, ending officially on 8 October. (Even then the area was not entirely quiet; the promising young poet Charles Sorley was killed near Hulluch on 13 October, in an attack on a position known as the Hairpin close to Hulluch.)

By the time that Blunden set off to join his battalion there were no major battles in the area and the front line was fairly settled. At one

Aerial view of Locon where Blunden joined the battalion in 1916; taken in 1918 by Thomas Armstrong, organist and later President of the Royal College of Music.

time, indeed, it was possible to buy the London daily papers, perhaps a day or two old, from a young French newsboy operating close to the front lines. This did not mean that occupation of the trenches was pleasant, however, for the ground lent itself to mining and counter-mining, and both the British and German tunnelling companies were frequently active in exploding mines of all sizes.

The 11th Royal Sussex was commanded by Lieutenant-Colonel H. J. Grisewood, with Major G. H. Harrison as second in command. Harrison became an admirer of Blunden's writing and also a firm friend.

George Harrison was one of the men with whom Blunden developed a deep and long-lasting friendship, recognising him as someone who appreciated his own approach to the war, his youth and sensitivity. Blunden wrote of him that 'his likeness cannot come again, in this life nor can man be more beloved' [U/W, p.145], a warm and revealing tribute to a man who was the nearest he had to a father-figure amongst his many military companions.

Recognising his young officer's literary talent, Harrison was to play a significant part in Blunden's military life in due course (see below).

Lt-Colonel George Harrison, DSO (Border Regt.). Officer commanding the 11th Btn Royal Sussex Regt. Originally appointed Second in Comand in May 1916, he took over command from Lieutenant-Colonel H J Grisewood in June 1916 and remained until his return to England in March 1917. Impressed by Blunden's success as a poet, he arranged his transfer to Battalion HQ as Field Works Officer. Blunden admired him deeply and remained in touch until Harrison's death in 1964 at the age of 86.

With the exception of a Christ's Hospital schoolfellow, 2nd Lieutenant Arnold Vidler, who had arrived a few days earlier, Blunden and another second lieutenant (Doogan, 'a plump, ironical unscareable Irishman') were the first officer reinforcements to reach the battalion since it reached France. Within a few hours of their arrival in the evening of 14 May 1916 the two young officers were sent from the battalion base at the farm in Le Touret to join the regular nightly ration party as it set out for the front line near Festubert. The chief incident of the day in the battalion had been one man killed at the morning 'stand to' and two other soldiers wounded during the day.

The journey began with supplies carried in

waggons and on limbers, with the two newcomers Blunden and Doogan at the middle of the column, 'with the mules behind us nosing forward, as if wishing to impart some experience to the novices'. [U/W, p.22]. After a while the rations and supplies were off-loaded onto trolleys, to be pushed along on a somewhat insecure narrow-gauge railway track to its terminus near the battalion headquarters, a dugout in a sand-bagged rampart. Here the new arrivals met their commanding officer, Lieutenant-Colonel Grisewood, his brother, 2nd Lieutenant Francis Grisewood, and the battalion adjutant.

Among other officers whom Blunden met at his posting was Captain Penruddocke, in charge of C Company in the Reserve line, 'rosy-faced, slender and argumentative', two years his senior, who was to be killed in action on the Somme. He is buried in Serre Road No. 2 British military cemetery.

This area around Festubert was to remain in Blunden's mind, and to appear in his conversations, many times over the coming years. Despite its ruined state he describes it as '... on the whole friendly to the fighting man', and his poem 'A House in Festubert' depicts the clashing contrast of the ruined houses in the midst of blossoming trees, the 'four lean guns' in conflict with

> the bird's call, the bee's hum,
> The sunbeams crossing the garden's shade

- observing, characteristically, how nature withstood the ravages of human effort. His future friends Siegfried Sassoon and Robert Graves had been here with the 1st Battalion Royal Welch Fusiliers about six months earlier, and their post-war memoirs offer vivid descriptions. Sassoon wrote about it being 'completely ruined by shell-fire' while

Graves's energetic, entertaining and somewhat wayward *Goodbye to All That* describes the village as 'a nightmare ever since the first fighting there in 1914'. In May 1916, it had not changed.

Blunden shows the British front line as appearing immensely old, like

Blunden's album, 'A House in Laventie, December 1915' with note: *Much like others at Richebourg etc. a little later (Mem. E W Tennant's Laventie poem).* **This comment refers to Edward Tennant's well-known poem** *'Home Thoughts in Laventie'* **which opens:**

> *'Green gardens in Laventie!*
> *Soldiers only know the street,*
> *Where the mud is churned and splashed about*
> *By battle-wending feet;*
> *And yet beside one stricken house there is a glimpse*
> *of grass, Look for it when you pass.'*

some survival from ancient history, and he was evidently much impressed by the many signs of lengthy warfare, with old uniforms and bones in the trenches, rats and skulls. The sight of a gun-emplacement strongly built in brick and cement indicated a long-term purpose about the place, with the continuous noise of artillery shells and small-arms fire emphasising the life he was joining. The ruined houses all had cellars which provided friendly shelter, and one such house was used as Advanced Brigade Headquarters, while a field battery of Divisional artillery was hidden behind a wooden fence painted to resemble a brick wall; this would open out for the battery to begin firing when required. The brewery just north of Festubert and mentioned by Sassoon ('Brewery Corner') was still in being, but suffered the occasional shell as the Germans knew that it was being used as an observation post.

On 22 May Blunden's friend Second Lieutenant E. X. Kapp went on patrol in No Man's Land. Kapp, a shrewd and interesting companion, was inclined to compose his autobiography, a good singer and skilled at charcoal drawings. He passed some critical remarks on verses composed by Blunden - whether or not it was as the result of these comments, when Blunden's poem ('The Festubert Shrine') reached publication in 1930 it showed several alterations from the version hand-written in his own copy of *Undertones of War* published two years earlier. But when Kapp left, he took with him Blunden's copy of the poems of John Clare. (U/W, p.40)

Proper trenches were not always possible, for the front line ran through marshy ground. A series of 'islands' or 'grouse butts' was built above ground, but as they consisted of nothing stouter than sandbags their apparent solidity gave a false sense of security. One of these overlooked the position known as 'Canadian Orchard', where the 1st Royal Welch had tried to hold on in May 1915.

To reach the front line, Blunden set off eastwards along the road from Festubert across the old German front line, towards La Quinque Rue.

Known to the British troops as 'Kinky Roo', this hamlet evidently impressed Blunden with its bare war-torn present appearance, and his own imaginings of the setting in peace-time. His poem 'La Quinque Rue' creates the bitter contrast between the sharp and noisy sights and sounds of war and his sense of trim quiet ordinary life in the farms, in other times. It opens:

O road in dizzy moonlight bleak and blue,
With forlorn effigies of farms besprawled,

With trees bitterly bare or snapped in two,
Why riddle me thus - attracted and appalled?

The road frequently came under enemy fire, so that the novice officer and his men had to drop down into the ditch. Their route took them south next, across a trench system known as 'Cover Trench' - in effect the real front line, for the land beyond was marked only by the 'Islands', some derelict and others continually manned. Canadian Orchard lay ahead, marking the limit of the British front line at this point. Ahead, the road led on across No Man's Land and the German trench system to the hamlet of Rue du Marais.

Lewis guns were used to stir up the German troops opposite Canadian Orchard, and Blunden suffered at one point from uncomfortably close retaliation into sandbags by his head. [U/W, 29] So recently the enthusiastic schoolboy, he was now undertaking his real military education; he learned where to post sentries, how to fire a flare, the importance of Vermoral Sprayers - a device to counteract gas, known as 'Immoral Sprayers'. *Undertones of War* speaks highly of his NCO, Sergeant Unstead, who acted as his guide and mentor.

Late in November 1915 Siegfried Sassoon had stopped in Festubert on his way to the trenches for a very welcome bowl of soup; six months later the spring nights were cold, and Blunden in his turn appreciated the soup kitchen which was still open there. It provided him with more than warming sustenance, for it was at the Festubert soup kitchen that he met 'a glorious fellow', Sergeant Frank Worley, who became a lifelong friend.

Like Colonel Harrison, Sergeant Worley became an enduring friend, and was appreciated for his unfailing good humour and courage. He knew how to comfort young soldiers under fire, and his trademark cry 'Come on, my lucky lads' was used by Blunden as the title of one of his strongest war poems, describing the cosmic scale and dazzling colours of war, the fury,

No. 555 Sgt. Frank Worley 11th Bn Royal Sussex Regt. 12 January 1917. Highly respected by Blunden, Worley came to the regiment from a butcher's shop in Sussex. Becoming expert in dealing with barbed wire, he became the battalion's Wiring Sergeant and often worked closely with Blunden, who considered that he should have received the VC. After the war Blunden lost track of him for many years, but they met again and remained firm friends.

The canal at Hinges (1920),
IWM Q37289

destruction and strangeness of combat - with, at the end, acceptance:

'It's plain we were born for this, naught else'

From his many grateful references to Worley's support, it is clear how important he was to Blunden's mental and physical survival. The two men lost sight of each other at the end of the war, as mentioned sadly in *Undertones of War* - but after its publication they met again and remained in touch. Despite his cheerful reliability Worley, who returned to shop-keeping, was afflicted by persistent war memories and never recovered fully from the strains of his war service. He died in 1954.

There was 'normal' daily 'wastage'. Blunden thought it was unnecessary for an officer holding captain's rank to inspect barbed wire in No Man's Land regularly - the nightly working parties often came under enemy fire, and there were frequent casualties. Perhaps as a farewell gesture, on 24 May 1916 the battalion decided to stir up the enemy. Artillery fire was called up, and a section of German trench opposite one of the 11th Royal Sussex's islands came under heavy fire in the afternoon.

Just before the 11th Royal Sussex departed for a rest period, Blunden was detailed to act as battalion billeting officer at their rest camp at Hingette. Before departing, he joined a group of officers from another company in a dugout where the company commander was less than welcoming; the young second lieutenant was addressed as 'that thing' – their officer casualties had been light and there was a 'wonderful superiority' among some of their remaining original

complement. [U/W p.36]. (He was not alone in this experience. Robert Graves similarly met with a cool welcome in July 1915, when he joined the 2nd Royal Welch Fusiliers at Laventie, a few miles to the north-west of Festubert, and had his revenge in the pages of *Goodbye to All That*.)

It was 25 May 1916 when Blunden and his billeting party left the battalion trenches at Festubert. Their first stop, after a long hot march, was at Hinges, a delightful change from the trenches, with orchards, barns, pollarded willows and undisturbed farm-land. [U/W, p.37] Many British battalions enjoyed these rural surroundings, either based in billets or marching through from 1915 right up to 1918.

Blunden and his party continued to nearby Hingette, to prepare for the battalion's arrival. In pleasing contrast with the recent encounter, the officer of the 1st Battalion Cambridgeshire Regiment from whom Blunden took over at Hinges was charming and cooperative. The battalion arrived next day, tired and weary after two or three weeks at the front, but training and inspections soon impinged on the brief rest, a mere three days. Blunden came to deplore the habitual petty militarism which prevented the troops from having adequate rest, in this case from a dangerous and demanding period in the Festubert trenches. The men's resentment on this occasion led to the signallers (who were usually regarded by the troops, perhaps not wholly justifiably, as enjoying congenial duties) acting in a remarkably unmilitary manner: they sent a 'round robin' protest to their commanding officer against the award of Field Punishment to one of

No. 1, Harley Street.

their section. At the ensuing battalion parade Colonel Grisewood made his anger and surprise very clear at this thoroughly unregimental act [U/W, p.38]

On Sunday 28 May the battalion took over from the 4th Battalion King's Liverpools, in reserve billets in Le Quesnoy. This small village lay to the east of Béthune and north of Beuvry, not far from the front

Canal d' Aire (La Bassée Canal). This sketch map shows Hinges, Hingette and Locon, with modern road numbers, to help the visitor explore Blunden's movements in 1916.

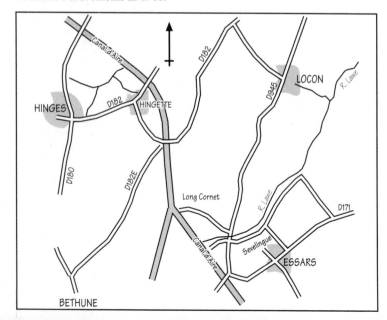

line at Cuinchy immediately south of the La Bassée canal.

Blunden was sent on a three-day course on gas in the little village of Essars [U/W, p.40]. The carefree and peaceful walk along the banks of the La Bassée canal to the Gas School must have been delightful, particularly to such a lover and observer of rural surroundings as the young Edmund Blunden. He recorded the clear water, the fish darting about in it; a Red Cross barge steaming by did not disturb the contented scene. Near the canal basin at Béthune the footpath led off across fields and through the village of Long Cornet, to the main road at Sevelingue; he was very conscious of the contrast between the stream of cars and lorries on this Béthune-Neuve Chapelle road and the luxuriance of the trees.

The village of Essars was, so far, unaffected by the war, and the Gas School was no more than a collection of huts. At lunch-time Blunden escaped to the even greater peace of the surrounding fields, to eat his army rations under a great willow-tree by one of the many dykes in this watery landscape. On another occasion he was able to discuss poetry with two officers (Hillier and Crockford) of the 39th Division's Pioneer battalion, the 13th (Forest of Dean) Battalion, Gloucestershire Regiment.

After the brief gas course Blunden's return to active warfare took him and his servant from rural peace to ruins. They walked eastwards from Essars on a sultry day, along the canal towpath and following the torn-up railway track to Cuinchy railway station and the damaged steel bridge at 'Pont Fixe' over the stagnant canal nearby. The two men turned right into Cuinchy's main street - known to the army as Harley Street - and reported to the Battalion HQ in a battered house not far away. The young poet was back in the war once more.

Once a flourishing village with railway station, post office, school, a brewery and various estaminets, by the time of Blunden's arrival Cuinchy was almost completely in ruins. In a pencilled addition to *Undertones of War* Blunden describes it as 'a yellow place, rank weeds and discoloured chalk'.

Village Line, the series of trenches that the battalion occupied, ran north-south parallel to Harley Street. Beyond them were the outskirts of Cuinchy, and to the east beyond it lay a brickfield, the region of the notorious brickstacks which were mostly held by the Germans.

Solid and sturdy, varying in height up to around 18 feet, compact in structure, each of the stacks covered an area of some 35 square feet. Dangerous winding tracks led through the stacks held by the British, along ground consisting of 'a wicked clay' [U/W, p.45]. The gaps between the stacks were always under enemy observation, and notice boards instructed troops to run between the safe points of shelter. It was not an attractive place:

> *Who that had been there for but a few hours could ever forget the sullen sorcery and mad lineaments of Cuinchy? A mining sector, as this was, never wholly lost the sense of hovering horror ... the ground became torn and vile, the poisonous breath of fresh explosions skulked all about it, and the mud which choked the narrow passages stank as one pulled through it ...* [U/W, p.48]

The Village Line ended, to the north, in the infamous La Bassée canal, and the British sector ran from the railway station near the Pont Fixe bridge to the brickstacks area, and included a large lock. The railway, on an embankment on the southern side of the canal - and therefore

Cuinchy railway station pictured in June 1917, showing a barricade across the railway line.

The railway at Cuinchy today.

within the same sector - was a dangerous spot, but sand-bagged culverts gave some protection from the frequent and effective enemy fire. At its southern end the Village Line ended at the main Cambrin - La Bassée road, running roughly parallel with the canal.

German and British miners were both at work beneath the line, and the whole area had a bad reputation. It was no surprise that when Blunden's friends Charlwood and Limbery-Buse - who knew the area - heard that the battalion was moving there, they exchanged 'doleful' smiles. Later that summer Charlwood decided that he would move on, and joined the Royal Flying Corps.

2nd Lieutenant Richard Limbery-Buse ('the Lumbering Bus') later followed a path that was noticeably different from that of either Charlwood or Blunden. Having left Tonbridge

School in 1910, he joined the Inns of Court O.T.C. just after the outbreak of war and was appointed a cadet on 18 November 1914. At the end of March 1915 he was commissioned into the 11th Royal Sussex Regiment, and accompanied it to France in March 1916. In September 1916 he was wounded and shell-shocked in the battalion's unsuccessful attack towards Beaumont Hamel, north of the River Ancre (see page 66), and was seconded to the Tank Corps in December 1916, returning to the 11th Royal Sussex in March 1917. While on six months' rest in England, beginning early in 1918, he was attached to the 52nd Battalion Royal Warwickshire Regiment until October 1918, when he joined the 2nd Battalion Royal Sussex Regiment in France. With them he was involved in the attack across the Sambre-Oise canal on 4 November 1918 at Catillon; he was wounded twice. In October 1919 he left the army and relinquished his commission in 1921. Later he went to live in California.

As well as the 11th Royal Sussex Headquarters, the many ruined buildings of Harley Street itself housed workshops and dressing-stations. The Battalion HQ, where Blunden reported, was in a sandbagged and barricaded villa, named 'Kingsclere', half-way along the road that ran south from the lock towards the ruined church at Cuinchy. Blunden found the cellar a welcome retreat from the fierce summer heat outside, and in addition it housed a piano. The trenches near the HQ were known to the British by easily memorable names, such as Sackville Street and Pudding Lane. Other pleasant names, such

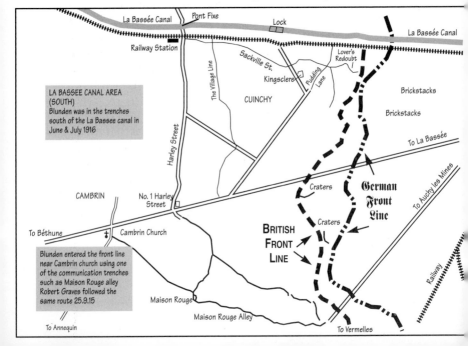

LA BASSEE CANAL AREA (SOUTH)
Blunden was in the trenches south of the La Bassee canal in June & July 1916

Blunden entered the front line near Cambrin church using one of the communication trenches such as Maison Rouge alley Robert Graves followed the same route 25.9.15

as Lover's Redoubt and Cabbage Patch Redoubt, belied their dangerous location.

Cuinchy Keep, near the ruined village church, was a strong-point which on the morning of Blunden's arrival had suffered heavy bombardment, some six hundred shells in an hour. On hearing this, Blunden

> *detachedly looked round for the dugout and made for it. That dugout was a deep one, with a steep mud-slide of an entrance; it was the smallest deep dugout that I ever saw, and yet it was friendly to us.* [U/W, p.43].

The battalion held the trench known as Esperanto Terrace, and suffered a stream of casualties from both raids and mining activity. Like many others, Blunden could never feel at ease around Cuinchy, and remarked on the atmosphere of foreboding and anxiety from his first entrance into Battalion HQ. Vigilance was evidently always necessary: on 4 June 1916 an enemy mine exploded at 8.45 pm only 25 yards from the battalion's trenches, killing six Other Ranks (including two brothers) and wounding 37 more. The battalion bombers immediately rushed forward and occupied the mine crater, despite heavy German artillery fire and a dilatory response from the British artillery, while a sap was dug out to it from the British trenches. A British mine was exploded north of the canal, in response, at 10.00 pm.

As his contribution to the battalion activities, Blunden applied himself to enlarging the trench map showing the British front lines and German front line trenches at a particular point. [U/W, p.44] A raid was proposed, with the 11th Royal Sussex responsible for attacking a heavily fortified section of the enemy line. The commanding officer, Lieutenant-Colonel Grisewood, was unhappy about the possible consequences of such an attack and firmly resisted it; the task was passed to another battalion, which suffered heavy casualties. As a result of his resistance, Grisewood relinquished his command of the battalion on 24 June 1916, a week before his brother, Second Lieutenant F. Grisewood, was killed in yet another abortive attack, this time near Neuve Chapelle, north of the canal.

Both sides were constantly engaged in mining. On 11 June a tunneller working in a British mine discovered a German mining shaft nearby; Blunden watched a sapper rushing past with a length of fuse, while Limbery-Buse went below ground into the gallery to see the Royal Engineer officer pull the detonating lever, exploding a defensive mine which destroyed the enemy mineworkings. The new crater was immediately raked by machine gun and rifle fire, but neither side

BRICKSTACK

The brickstacks. (IWM Q 56232)

wanted possession of it, and the fighting and firing eventually petered out. Two hours later the 11th Royal Sussex were relieved by the 2nd Battalion Argyll and Sutherland Highlanders, and marched away out of the line to billets at Hingette.

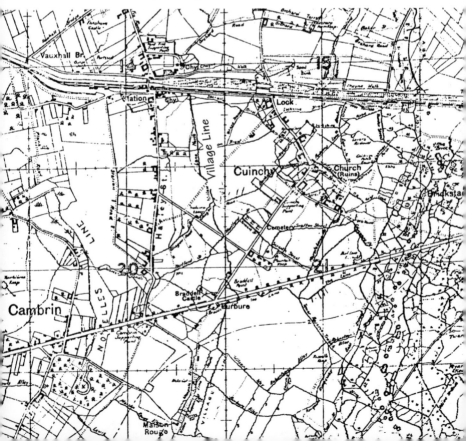

The rest was a brief one, and by 16 June 1916 they were on the march to Croix Barbée, a little village just north of Richebourg, where they took over from the 14th Battalion Gloucestershire Regiment in reserve. A diversion was needed on the nearby front, to prevent enemy reinforcements being sent to meet the forthcoming British attack on 1 July, on the Somme, and the plan included the 11th Royal Sussex. Still smarting somewhat after severe admonitions from the adjutant - for mounting a guard considered lacking in military smartness - Blunden discovered that he had been ordered away to a little village with the delightful name of Le Paradis.

Here, in the outbuildings of a château, he took charge of the stock of explosives and supplies left by an army bombing school which had recently closed down. His time here was very agreeable, in the care of the courteous elderly owner and his two daughters who spoke of the hand-to-hand fighting they had seen in the château grounds early in the war. The front line was later pushed eastwards, but Blunden could see the nightly flares, red, white and green, rising and falling away to the east towards the Aubers Ridge (U/W, p.53).

This period was over too soon, and Blunden rejoined the 11th Royal Sussex near Richebourg. Despite heavy artillery bombardment, the poet hidden beneath the officer's uniform noted the surviving gardens and the many wayside shrines. (As an officer, however, he also commented on the apparent nervousness of the Royal Engineer officers who supervised the trench building.) He ran into a dangerous moment with two sergeants, Bodle and May: exploring a trench, they were out long enough to have been forgotten by the sentries, and were fired on as they returned to the British lines, though without being hit (in 1918, Siegfried Sassoon suffered the same experience, although in his case he suffered a minor wound).

'The Guard's Mistake' (also known as 'The Sentry's Mistake') This humorous and observant poem refers to an episode at Richebourg St Vaast, perhaps the reprimand noted above. Giving free rein to his usual keen eye for the detail and incident of rural life, Blunden describes a peaceful setting:

> Round the still quadrangle of the empty farm
> The company soon had settled their new home;
> The cherry-boughs were beckoning every arm,
> The stream ran wrinkling by with playful foam,
> And when the guard was at the gateway set,
> Surrounding pastoral sweetly stole their wit.

- and the guard set by the road consisted of a 'cowman', armed only with a cudgel, who stood smiling, comfortable

and proprietoral. The sting comes in the last four lines:
But now a flagged car came ill-omened there.
The crimson-mottled monarch, shocked and shrill,
Sent our poor sentry scampering for his gun,
Made him once more 'the terror of the Hun.'

There is more in the narrative of this poem for the soldier-reader than for other readers; others may simply smile at a pompous staff officer reprimanding an unmilitary-looking sentry - but the arrival of a staff car with senior officer in itself meant serious business in preparation, while 'ill-omened' foreshadows the result of his plans. As so often, Blunden is writing for those in a position to understand a grim truth behind the gentle pastoral opening.

The end of June found Blunden at a post near Neuve Chapelle, beside the junction of the Estaires – La Bassée road with the Armentières – Béthune roads, a site with a discouraging war history which seemed unlikely to change. Early in the war, a battered semi-circular web of trenches here had become known as Port Arthur; fighting was fierce in October 1914, almost continuous with heavy casualties, when the British and German trenches were only 50 yards apart. The area saw further very heavy fighting in March 1915, during the battle of Neuve Chapelle, and more was to come.

Blunden was not the only member of the British Army in this area who later became famous for his creative talents. The former student at the Royal College of Music, Ivor Gurney, held the line near here with his comrades in the 2/5th Glosters for a week in 1916, at a point where the opposing trenches were so close that bombs could easily be thrown from one side to the other. Gurney's poetry (which he turned to in the trenches because it was impossible to compose music in such circumstances) was barely known by his fellow-soldiers, but his poems written about this place speak warmly of the comradeship that he found here. And in March that year David Jones, painter and poet, was close to the Port Arthur crossroads (at a strong-point called Pioneer Keep), with the London Welch. In his long prose poem 'In Parenthesis', Jones gives a brief but vivid description of the death of a Brigade staff officer, killed when a shell burst on the nearby fire trench. Jones indicates surprise that a staff officer should be so close to the fighting.

Notes & Sources
Desmond Graham, *The Truth of War: Owen, Blunden and Rosenberg,* Carcanet, 1984

Chapter Three

'SHARPLY BOMBARDED AT ALL HOURS'
[U/W, P.72]

The expected diversionary attack, engaging German troops which might otherwise have moved to withstand the Somme offensive, began on 30 June 1916. Blunden was excluded from taking part, but some men of his battalion were required as carrying parties, bringing up small arms ammunition and material for the Royal Engineers in support of the attacking battalions, the 12th and 13th Royal Sussex and the 14th Hampshires. Their objective was the enemy front line, known as 'the Boar's Head' on account of its odd configuration, south-west of Neuve Chapelle.

This attack was described by Blunden as a massacre. The British troops met devastating German fire, not least as the troops tried to negotiate a muddy ditch in their path which was some 14 feet wide and three feet deep. Some of the stragglers from the 11th Royal Sussex carrying parties returned to Blunden's dug-out at Port Arthur exhausted, their uniforms and equipment torn by bullets. British casualties were heavy (122 in the 11th Royal Sussex alone) and included the young brother of Lieutenant-Colonel Grisewood, who had relinquished command of the battalion six days earlier, and Sergeant May, one of the two who had accompanied Blunden a few days earlier as they crawled out along the 'digging'. There were dead men to be buried and discarded equipment to be salvaged: but the dead in No Man's Land were out of reach, and at least one battalion history remarks on the way the dead lay in rows, indicating how they had been scythed down by German machine-gun fire. Blunden's sober comment in *Undertones of War,* looking back as he wrote it several years later, was:

Edmund Blunden, photographed at Poperinghe in 1916.

> So the attack on the Boar's Head closed, and so closed the
> admirable youth or maturity of many a Sussex and Hampshire
> worthy.

The effects of war on the main street in Givenchy-lez-La Bassée

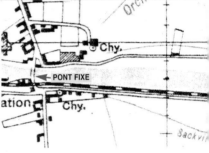

The survivors were relieved by the 6th Battalion Cheshire Regiment, which Blunden would encounter again in the future, and returned to rest billets at Kings Road, Le Touret, on 2 July. 'Rest', however, was an illusion, for the battalion was involved in the usual behind-the-line activities - physical exercises, drills and route marches. The day after they reached the rest billets the men who had taken part in the disastrous attack on the Boar's Head trenches were inspected by the Corps Commander at 10.30 a.m., and by the Divisional Commander fifteen minutes later, with a battalion inspection by the C.O., Major Harrison, the same evening: another example, in Blunden's eyes, of 'eyewash', the unnecessary military activity (at least all on the same day) that always followed the exertions of front-line duty. A more agreeable episode was to march to Vieille Chapelle, a few miles to the north of Le Touret, for very welcome baths.

On 6 July the battalion was on the move again, this time for the Auchy-les-Mines sector via Beuvry and Cambrin, not far from the Cuinchy front and the ill-famed Brickstacks. On 8 July the 11th Royal Sussex entered the trench system beside Cambrin church, which was being used as a dressing station [U/W, p.65]. Many of the long communication trenches leading up to front-line positions were lined with brick.

Robert Graves had been here nearly a year earlier, in September

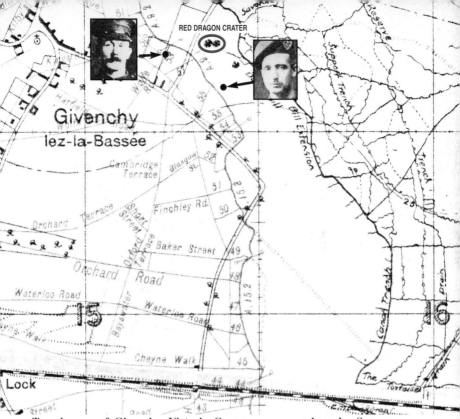

Trench map of Givenchy. Victoria Crosses were won here by Sapper Hackett (left) and Sergeant Erskine (right). See page 53

1915, with the 2nd Battalion Royal Welch Fusiliers at the opening of the Battle of Loos and in particular the disastrous attack towards the railway lines in front of Auchy-les-Mines. As he went up to the firing line from a position known as Maison Rouge Alley, just in front of Cambrin church, he too had to negotiate a communication trench said to be about half a mile long. The attack by Graves's battalion in support of the 1st Battalion Middlesex Regiment was very costly: the Brigade lost 40 officers and 800 men shot down in the first five minutes of the attack. Graves was in the front line, ready to lead his company forward, when fortunately the order to advance was cancelled.

In contrast, by the early hours of 8 July 1916 the 11th Royal Sussex had reached these front line trenches at the cost of three casualties. As Blunden looked over No Man's Land he noted that the British front was dominated by Auchy on the higher ground opposite. The battalion was soon in action: a British mine was exploded in No Man's Land at midnight, and the battalion sappers immediately dug out towards to the crater to occupy the near lip formed by material blasted up by the explosion and offering a useful height advantage. (Mines were

41

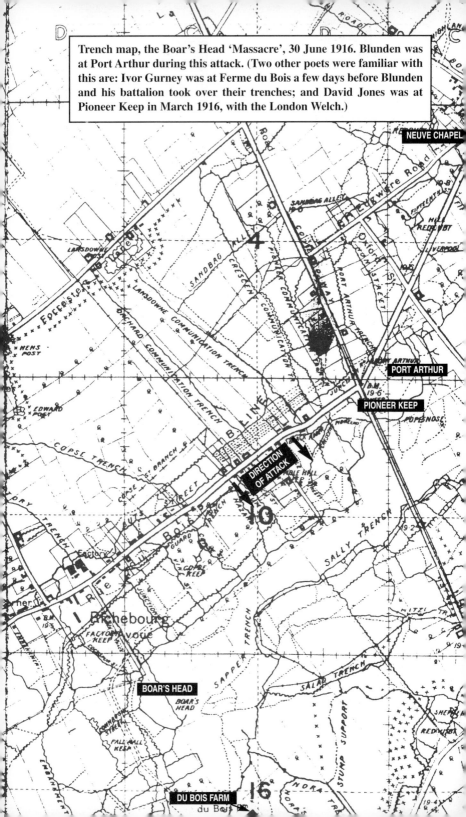

Trench map, the Boar's Head 'Massacre', 30 June 1916. Blunden was at Port Arthur during this attack. (Two other poets were familiar with this are: Ivor Gurney was at Ferme du Bois a few days before Blunden and his battalion took over their trenches; and David Jones was at Pioneer Keep in March 1916, with the London Welch.)

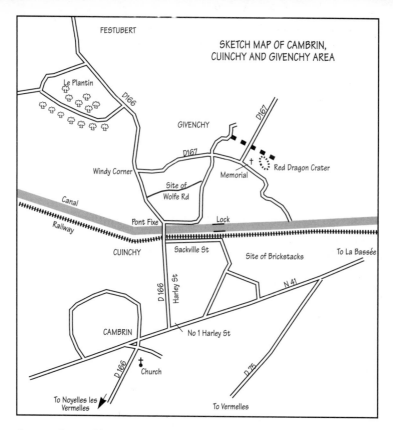

SKETCH MAP OF CAMBRIN,
CUINCHY AND GIVENCHY AREA

frequently used in this way, by both sides.)

The remaining few days in the line brought several casualties. Second Lieutenant Doogan, who joined the battalion with Blunden, was wounded, and survived; but a cheerful young lance-corporal was killed, his remains seen almost immediately afterwards by his brother who happened to come round the traverse in the trench. The 11th Royal Sussex's method of recruitment actively encouraged brothers to join up together and Blunden had previously remarked on the family tragedy created in this way: when the battalion was occupying the Brickstacks trench line at Cuinchy he had been deeply struck by the misery of a boy standing by a stretcher where his brother, severely wounded, was waiting to be carried down to the dressing station.

Deaths continued, almost casually, with a sentry shot through the head as he looked through a loophole and seven stretcher bearers killed by rifle-grenade fire which hit their exposed shelter. Late in the evening of 10 July a patrol went over into No Man's Land to examine a railway line running across it - one of the objectives which Robert Graves's Royal Welch failed to reach on 25 September 1915 and evidently still uncaptured ten months later. Intense activity continued on both sides, with a German mine detonated on 13 July close to the battalion's right front and heavy shelling from both sides, ranging from rifle grenades through to heavy-calibre shells.

Blunden, who commented drily that the Cambrin sector was 'beginning to terrify', must have been relieved to move out the next day, to Beuvry. They lined up on the paved road, ready to move on 'under arches of rippling leafage', as Blunden noted by hand in the margin of *Undertones of War,* when they were astonished at the sight of the transport provided: old London buses, 'disguised with drab paint'. They boarded thankfully, and settled once more into the billets at Kings Road, Le Touret.

The good news there was that Second Lieutenant Doogan was back on duty, healed from his wound. The bad news was that out-of-line activities were to begin, the familiar tedious round of drills, inspections and working parties.

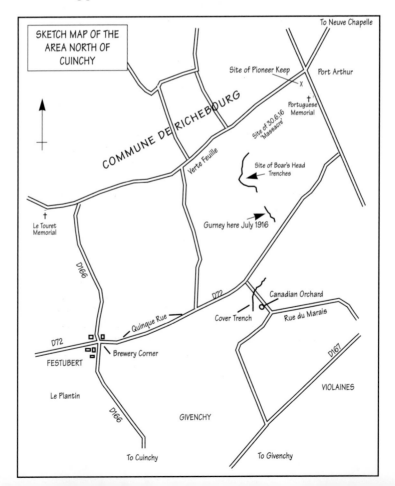

The worst news, on 19 July 1916, after a mere four days out of the line, was that the battalion was under orders to take over a different part of the front. This was near the Boar's Head trenches, where the 11th Royal Sussex had suffered so badly and so recently (30 June). The precise location was just south of the Boar's Head, known as the Ferme du Bois from a farm of that name in the German lines. The trenches here, taken over by the Royal Sussex late on the night of 20th July, had been relinquished a few days earlier when the 2/5th Glosters - including the musician/poet Ivor Gurney - moved to the Laventie area for what later proved to be yet another bloody and disastrous attack on Aubers Ridge.

The attack on the Boar's Head, which led to the 'massacre' commented on by Blunden on 30 June, was required for the same reason as the attack on 19 July 1916 in which Ivor Gurney's battalion was involved - to prevent enemy reinforcements leaving for the Somme. The local objective was the capture of Fromelles; the Official History states that the operation was 'intended to hold the enemy to his ground and to teach him that he could not with impunity reinforce the main battle by thinning his line'. As Blunden wrote, the undertaking was 'without the least success' and a cause for 'some bitter jesting'. 'The name most disgustfully mentioned,' he later commented privately, 'was that of General Haking'.

Despite courage and élan, the attack on Fromelles by the 61st Division (which included the Glosters) and the 5th Australian Division was a failure, with heavy casualties: the Australians lost 5,533 men and the British 1,547. Lives were saved by the humanity of the Germans who proposed a truce so that the dead and wounded could be collected, and for three days stretcher bearers and others covered No Man's Land to bring in dead and wounded.

Literary networks: In later years Blunden visited Ivor Gurney in the mental hospital in Kent where he spent the final years of his life. As the battlefield was being cleared in 1916, another future friend was in great danger, and indeed given up for dead - this was Robert Graves, lying severely wounded near Mametz Wood on the Somme. His war experiences left their mark, both physical and emotional, and a decade later Blunden (and Sassoon) fell out with Graves over episodes in his war memoirs *Goodbye to All That*. In the long run, however, both men felt that they had somewhat over-reacted to Graves's sardonic account of his life at the front.

LA BASSÉE ROAD

HARLEY ST (Cuinchy)

Pages from Blunden's album (continued on page 48) with his own captions. The building on the left at the road junction (below left) is probably No.1 Harley Street, used as a Dressing Station during the war; the road running left-right is the Béthune-La Bassée road, now the N 41.

CAMBRIN

CAMBRIN

FROM ANNEQUIN FOSSE
eastward

Typical "just
behind"

Blunden, meanwhile, was sent with his platoon on detached duty from the Ferme du Bois lines, to trenches within a couple of miles of the Fromelles battlefield at Port Arthur, familiar from the recent past and the Boar's Head 'massacre' at the end of June. Here, in a ruined brewery, he, his much-admired friend Sergeant Worley and the platoon occupied a cellar in comparative comfort. Blunden describes the place:

> The queer, disabled building was encircled with sandbag ramparts, a map of the whole looking like a diagram of the intestines. In the large cellars there was room for forty men or so; the officer had a side cellar to himself, with a sound bed, and a private stock of new sandbags for bedclothes. Opposite this unsafe but habitually trusted burrow was a little outhouse turned into a machine-gun position, with a store-room; and thence some mole of an engineer, but hopeful beyond good sense, had hollowed out a low tunnel, a secret passage, which led into the communication trench, Hun Street, some way off. ... Near by was a pit, the result of much sandbag filling; among its broken spades and empty tins I found a pair of boots, still containing someone's feet [U/W, p.71].

> (Twenty-five years later Blunden felt that he still haunted Port Arthur, and wondered whether the establishment was still aware of his presence.)

Blunden himself had the use of the side cellar with its bed and sandbag bedding. They were surrounded by piles of bully beef tins of various brands, and worked through them to decide which was best. Despite these comforts, they were under bombardment at all hours. Among those who suffered severe wounds (on 21 July) was Private Nice, a 16-year-old who had somehow managed to get to France, and the adjutant and his runner who were on their way to inspect Blunden's post. The experience of receiving instructions from the adjutant, who thought he was dying, deeply impressed Blunden with a profound sense of the abnormality of the world in which such incidents were part of everyday life. Soon after this Blunden and his men returned to their unit, now in the British lines east of Festubert [U/W, p.72].

In the midst of the abnormality and disruption of war, Blunden was becoming somewhat foolhardy, perhaps strained by exposure to front line conditions. Back in their familiar Festubert area he risked sniper fire to reach men in the dreaded Islands, the lonely sandbagged strong-points built above the water-logged ground and sometimes known as 'grouse butts'. After delivering materials required there he explored parts of No Man's Land and returned with a number of abandoned rifles and helmets - including, 'in the bliss of ignorance', some unexploded German bombs.

> *Our colonel, Harrison, who followed me in the daylight route to the Islands, met me after such an occasion, frightening me greatly. He looked at my collection, and asked, 'Been big-game hunting?' but I was tongue-tied, as I had once in Richebourg village, where he .... asked me which post I had been holding, 'Port Arthur' would not come; I stood striving for speech; he smiled, and I ruefully asked my nearest man* [U/W, p.74].

For someone who took delight in conversation, language, debate and quick turn of phrase, such failures must have been disconcerting and uncomfortable; the mature poet and writer tells the anecdote with humour, but the strain underlying it must have been felt once more, ten years later, as he wrote about his 19-year-old self.

GERMAN FRONT LINE

The Locks at Cuinchy on the La Bassée Canal looking towards the German Front Lines. The locks were in the British Support Line and sometimes came under enemy fire as the German lines were just round the bend in the canal. The British troops used the lock's water for bathing, ignoring the danger from German artillery fire. Another bathing hazard was the maze of signal cables crossing the canal but strewn below the water's surface. It was somewhere on the bank on the left of the photograph that the Germans made an attempt to fraternise, resulting in the threat of Court Martial to 2nd Lts. Cassels and Redway.

PONT FIXE

GIVENCHY

The pattern of life here was dangerous, full of minor incident, and easily confusing. Night patrols could end in muddle, as the quantity of metal in the ground distorted compasses and disorientated the patrol. Mistaken identity was another hazard; Blunden had already experienced this in June, and now the 13th Royal Sussex suffered severely when a patrol was completely lost and was fired at by men of their own battalion. More than a dozen men were killed or wounded. The unfortunate officer in command, McNaughton, was described by Blunden as temperamentally 'suited for a quiet country parsonage and would usually have mislaid his spectacles.' The ill-luck of the 13th Royal Sussex continued when one of their men was killed as they relieved Blunden's 11th on 28 July 1916.

Rest for the 11th Royal Sussex was in billets at Le Touret once more and, as usual, brought the usual round of kit inspections, working parties and physical exercises, this time with the addition of riding lessons for officers. They moved from Le Touret, and marched north to La Couture before moving on to the outskirts of Béthune. The next few days were occupied with route marches, bathing in the canal and inspections, by the Brigade Commander, Brigadier-General M. L. Hornby and then by the General Officer commanding the Division.

A few days later, on 6 August, the battalion paraded in the Great Square at Béthune, part of a ceremonial church parade to mark the second anniversary of the war, before marching off beside the canal to Givenchy. They took over their sector of trenches late in the evening from the outgoing Sherwood Foresters, at the cost of one man wounded. The march eastwards along the canal towards Cuinchy was pleasant, even though the prospect of the trenches was less so. Blunden, his eye ever alert in rural surroundings, recorded the drowsy summer setting and the long weedy growth in the canal, an army diver exploring a sunken barge, and then hulks of barges in broad pools. They reached the 'crumpled bridge' at Cuinchy - known to the troops as Pont Fixe - and, instead of crossing the bridge and heading into the trench lines near the Brickstacks as in May, turned north to a large canal lock which barred the waterway at the British Support Line. They were in the Givenchy front - the Right Sector - and would spend six days here [U/W, p.77].

On their march they saw junctions and communication trenches with pleasant English names - Windy Corner, Queen's Road, Orchard Road, Wolfe Road, Hatfield Road; and the trench line known as the Duck's Bill. Blunden was to remember this spot.

Two pieces of good fortune awaited Blunden here while he was lodged in one of the ruined houses where Wolfe Road crossed a street running north from the lock into Givenchy village, with white shutters and painted railings still noticeable. First, he had a narrow escape when a 'short' from a British artillery battery landed in the ground beside the window and the shell's nosecap buried itself in the wallpaper; and then he was visited by the battalion's Commanding Officer, Lieutenant-Colonel Harrison: before his departure for France, Blunden had left 'a trifling collection of verses' with a London publisher, and Colonel Harrison had read the 'kind review' that appeared in the *Times Literary Supplement.*

This casual coincidence in his colonel's leisure reading was to change Blunden's military career and possibly save his life, for it took the unimportant subaltern away to Battalion HQ and made him the 'Field Works Officer'. Colonel Harrison was 'overjoyed to have an actual author in his battalion'; the young writer was summoned to

The Givenchy Sector. Blunden was here early in August 1916, holding the line before going to the Somme. It was at the Red Dragon Crater that Blunden was criticised by a senior officer for carrying out manual work.

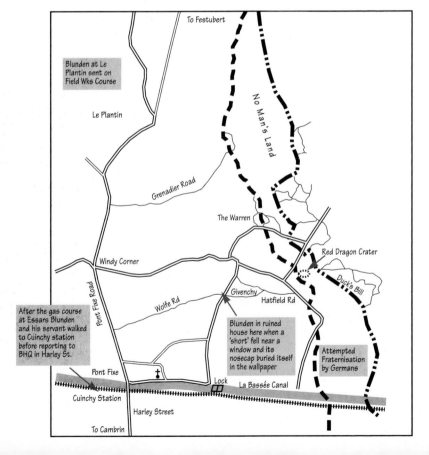

To Festubert

Blunden at Le Plantin sent on Field Wks Course

Le Plantin

No Man's Land

Grenadier Road

The Warren

Red Dragon Crater

Windy Corner

Duck's Bill

Pont Fixe Road

Wolfe Rd

Givenchy
Hatfield Rd

After the gas course at Essars Blunden and his servant walked to Cuinchy station before reporting to BHQ in Harley St.

Blunden in ruined house here when a 'short' fell near a window and its nosecap buried itself in the wallpaper

Attempted Fraternisation by Germans

Pont Fixe

Lock   La Bassée Canal

Cuinchy Station

Harley Street

To Cambrin

dinner in his commanding officer's presence that night, awed and impressed by the company and the fine glass that they used.

He was given a variety of 'odd jobs' to do, concerning a large mine crater known as the Red Dragon Crater. It lay near the section of the front line known from its configuration as the Duck's Bill, and when first created by the explosion of a German mine on 22 June 1916 it was called the Duck's Bill Crater. The drama of that occasion and the history of that short front-line area explain the change of name.

Red Dragon Crater: The 2nd Royal Welch Fusiliers took over the section on 21 June 1916. At 2 a.m. the next morning the German mine exploded directly under their B Company, which lost two-thirds of its strength, including two officers and its C.S.M. The resulting crater measured 120 yards long by 70 feet wide, 30 feet deep, and was the largest crater on the Western Front at the time. Oddly enough the detonation was not felt at all at Windy Corner, Givenchy (the battalion H.Q.), but Division H.Q. in Béthune heard it and signalled for details.

The 2nd Royal Welch was a regular battalion and still had many of its pre-war NCOs and men. They reacted promptly and repulsed German raids following the explosion. Among those who distinguished themselves that day was Captain, formerly Sergeant-Major, Stanway: two weeks later he was promoted to the rank of Lieutenant-Colonel and given command of the 6th Battalion Cheshire Regiment (a territorial force battalion), a great achievement for someone who had been a Company Sergeant Major less than two years earlier.

Just at the time when the German mine exploded, the British 254 Tunnelling Company was digging a mine-shaft towards the German line near the Duck's Bill trenches. The detonation of the German mine blocked the gallery, burying some of the miners; several tunnellers were rescued, but one, Sapper Hackett, refused to leave a wounded comrade. For four days rescuers struggled to reach them in their blocked gallery - but without success. Sapper Hackett received a posthumous Victoria Cross for his self-sacrifice.

William Hackett.

Another V.C. was won at the same site on the same day, by Sergeant J. Erskine of the 5th Cameronians, for going into No Man's Land and bringing in men wounded in the mine explosion. As for the Royal Welch, their prompt action in defeating an enemy raiding force of some 150 men brought them generous compliments; and the name of 'Red Dragon', from the design of their regimental cap badge, became the official name of the crater.

John Erskine.

Blunden had already met the 6th Cheshires when they relieved the 11th Royal Sussex at the Boar's Head early in June, and he was to meet them again later in the year on the Somme. His next task, on 7 August, was to restore the sap destroyed by the heavy German artillery fire on the Red Dragon Crater (typically described in terms of its brookside setting beneath some shell-damaged trees). To his surprise the working party consisted of 100 men, including his NCO friend Sergeant Worley, transferred to Battalion H.Q. as wiring sergeant. They completed the task, not without a reprimand for Blunden, for carrying a duckboard under his arm: manual work was not appropriate for officers, whose job is to direct and supervise. Despite this firm reminder he returned from time to time, to tidy up the operation. On 10 August his friend 2nd Lieutenant Lintott went up to inspect their progress, unfortunately coinciding with a mortar barrage that nearly buried him. The idea of further improvements was abandoned.

Despite the discomforts and dangers of service in the trenches round Givenchy, Blunden's memories of the area had 'an Arcadian quality about them' [U/W, p.80]. He could send his batman to the rear and have him return within two hours with a sandbag holding beer and chocolate; and, important to the country lad with a passion for everything to do with water, he could look into the weeds in the canal and see great quantities of pike. The canal had other uses, of greater value to the troops: bathing parties could swim in the lock, despite occasional enemy shell-fire and the presence of army signallers' cables.

A more morally testing problem arose in August when, as the battalion diary records, 'at 5.45 a.m. 9th August 1916 the enemy showed himself in many places along our front and attempted overtures with our men'. Two British officers, named privately by Blunden as Second Lieutenants Cassels and Redway, gave orders not to fire on a German officer and his men who appeared from their trench and tried to fraternise with the British, possibly in the hope of identifying the unit for their own Intelligence services. Cassels and Redway were placed under open arrest; Redway was sent out late the same night in a fighting patrol, to attack a German working party. He returned safely, but several of the patrol did not. The incident and military misdemeanour did not appear to disrupt their army careers severely, for Cassels was awarded the Military Cross two months later.

Further south the Battle of the Somme was raging, and when the 11th Royal Sussex's stint in the Givenchy line came to an end on 11 August (they handed over to the 18th King's Liverpools), the Division was summoned to move. More troops were needed on the Somme battlefield; General Joffre was by no means satisfied with the development of the offensive, and criticised the apparently endless series of minor attacks. He hoped for future attacks to be made on a wider front, to make progress on the western front and to help the Russians effectively by making it impossible for German troops to be moved to the eastern front. The 11th Sussex were to form a very minor element in this grand strategy.

Despite the Boar's Head and the continuing casualties and dangers, Blunden felt that he had no conception of the realities of the Somme offensive. The imminent change seemed to produce 'a kind of holiday feeling' among the battalion - presumably the mere prospect of a change was welcome. But in his poem 'Two Voices', Blunden expresses in his quiet oblique manner how the announcement of going south to the Somme was greeted as 'death-news', and the three stanzas end with an air of foreboding. This darker reaction was more realistic, and many of the battalion were to lose their lives.

For Blunden, the late spring and early summer months of 1916 were an introduction to a peculiar form of adult life - the distinctive combination of boredom, danger and ruin that made up so much of the Great War, in which he nevertheless found glimpses of rural beauty. As he delighted in these sights, he clung almost desperately to the reassurance of normality, the true features of real life.

Sometimes with his battalion, sometimes on a course or posted separately with his company, he became familiar with quiet corners and backwaters round Festubert, Cuinchy, La Bassée and its canal - low-lying, with few distinctive physical features, easy to cross in later times in twenty minutes' driving. Poems grew out of these wearisome weeks, reflecting the sudden dangers and the growing friendships, reliance on others and understanding of human nature under strain and distress.

> *Some found an owl's nest in the hollow skull*
> *Of the first pollard from the malthouse wall;*
> *Some hurried through the swarming sedge*
> *About the ballast-pond's green edge,*
> *And flashed through sunny deeps like boys from school;*
> *All was discovery, love and laughter all.*

from 'Battalion in Rest'

Visit: Cambrin is easily reached from the A 26 motorway (exit no. 6) towards Béthune and the N 41 La Bassée road. In Cambrin, turn right along the D 166 and park near the church, on the left. It was here early

in July 1916 that, marching into the nearby trenches, Blunden found that the church was in use as a dressing station. The cemetery extension behind the church holds some 1,200 British graves, as well as 150 French and three German burials.

Being close to the front lines, it includes many graves grouped by battalions that were involved in the battles of Loos in 1915.

Return to the car and continue past the church to the traffic lights. Turn right, onto the N 41 again. At the next crossroads turn left into the Rue Anatole France, known to the British army as Harley Street - the first house on the right was well known to Blunden as No. 1 Harley Street. In June 1916 the street was full of ruined houses in use for military purposes (including dressing stations) and was familiar to Blunden.

At the far end of the street, just before the bridge across the canal, note Cuinchy Railway Station to the left beside the canal; Blunden and his servant walked along the railway track to rejoin the battalion after the course at Essars Gas School in June 1916. Take a sharp turn to the right here, so that the La Bassée canal and the railway are on your left; as the road bears to the right along this road, the house

Cambrin Church, 1998. When Blunden entered the front line trenches nearby in July 1916, it was being used as a Dressing Station. Robert Graves was also here, in September 1915.

known as 'Kingsclere' would have been on the right, used by most units as a battalion HQ. At the T junction turn right, then a few yards further on turn sharp left: this leads through the area known as The Brickstacks to the N 41. Turn right along to the next crossroads and turn right into Harley Street again.

Repeat your route up the street to the railway station on the left, but this time go straight ahead across the canal bridge, known to Blunden as 'Pont Fixe', and turn right immediately beyond it, down the road to the lock buildings. This is where the men of the Royal Sussex used to bathe, despite the festoons of engineers' cables both above and below the water.

Communication trenches were constructed on the left of this road, with two, Orchard Road and Wolfe Road, coming in from the left. It was in a room in a house on this road, whilst Blunden was in occupation, that the nosecap from a 'short' buried itself in the wallpaper [see p.52]. Near here, on the right, was the spot where German soldiers tried to fraternise with the Royal Sussex in the British front line on 9 August 1916.

Turn right at the T-junction, leading to the prominent divisional memorial on the corner of the D 167, to the West Lancashires. Park here, and walk a short way to the right, along the D 167. The Red

56

Dragon Crater lay in the field on the right near the road. It was here, in August 1916, that Blunden was in charge of a working party to restore a destroyed sap.

Turn and drive back towards the canal, but instead of turning to the left to Cuinchy carry on to the junction where the road joins the D 166 Cuinchy - Festubert road, a junction known as 'Windy Corner'. Turn right here, on to the D 166.

Follow the road for about half a mile, and just past the Festubert village sign turn left into Rue Capitte (a minor road with a weight limit sign). Stop after about half a mile, by a small group of houses: this is Le Plantin, a very peaceful area of woodland and water. Several bunkers are clearly visible behind the houses on the left.

Le Plantin was where Blunden attended a trench-building course in July 1916 (see p.60). (It appears that during the Second World War a French pilot serving in the R.A.F. would sometimes fly low over his parents' house here as a kind of recognition salute.)

Continue to the T-junction and turn right, passing the British cemetery (Brown's Road) on the left, then turn left on the D 166. At the crossroads turn right on the D 72, the Rue de Lille. This turning was known to Siegfried Sassoon as Brewery Corner when he was there in November 1915 with the Royal Welch Fusiliers. After about 1.5 mile, turn right into the Rue de l'Etang and stop the car after about 100 yards: this is approximately where Cover Trench crossed the road when Blunden was in the line at Canadian Orchard (further down the road, on the left).

Reverse direction and return to the D 72, turning right along it. After about three-quarters of a mile an 'L'-shaped block of woodland set back from the road on the left marks the site of the Ferme du Bois; both Edmund Blunden and Ivor Gurney occupied the British lines in front of this farm in July 1916. Shortly beyond this, turn left on the busy D 947, continue past the Portuguese Cemetery and then the Indian Memorial on the left. Blunden was in this area (Port Arthur), on several occasions.

Continue along the D 947 and take the second turn on the right (Le Pont Logis) on to the D 170. The road soon joins a long straight section of the D 171 where, on the right, both David Jones (London Welch) and Ivor Gurney (2/5th Glosters) saw action during the summer of 1916.

Turn left along the D 171 through Fauquissart, on to Le Picantin and then Petillon; Gurney was in action between Le Picantin and the cross-roads at Petillon in July 1916. Take the right turn at this cross-roads on to the D 175 (rue Delva) and drive down as far as the cemetery - V.C.Corner Australian cemetery; park the car at the Fromelles Memorial park just beyond it (this newly cleared area has bunkers, and a striking recent statue of an Australian soldier rescuing a comrade).

The field opposite the cemetery is the site of the Sugar Loaf where, following the fierce British and Australian attack on 19th July 1916, the Germans declared a brief armistice so that the dead and wounded

CAMBRIN CHURCH
Aug. 1915 & much
as we saw it in June '16.

CAMBRIN CHURCH
Here we halted on our way to
a trench relief, summer even

Cambrin Church 1915, two views (above) from Edmund Blunden's album, with his captions. The modern pictures show the same views today.

could be cleared from the battlefield; Gurney's battalion took part in the clearance. Unusually, this British cemetery is entirely a mass grave.

Turn the car and drive back along the D 175, turning left on to the D 171 through Neuve Chapelle to the junction at Port Arthur once more. Go across, past the Indian memorial (well worth a visit). Just past it, on the left, was Pioneer Keep, referred to by David Jones in 'In Parenthesis'; and a few hundred yards further on, on the left of the road, is the site of what Blunden called the 'massacre' of 30 June 1916, the Boar's Head.

Continue straight ahead for about 2.5 miles to the memorial on the left of the road at Le Touret. This commemorates the deaths of British and Canadian soldiers killed in 1914 and 1915 in the battles of La Bassée, Neuve Chapelle, Aubers Ridge and Festubert. Sassoon was also here in November 1915, and Blunden in the summer of 1916.

Continue again along the D 171 to Essars, where Blunden attended a course of instruction on dealing with poison gas. Afterwards, he and his servant walked along the banks of the La Bassée canal to rejoin the 11th Royal Sussex at Cuinchy, and the dreaded Brickstacks.

To rejoin the A 26 motorway at Junction 6, carry on along the D 171 and follow signs round Béthune.

Notes & Sources
David Jones, *In Parenthesis*, Faber, 1937
Robert Graves, *Goodbye to All That*, Penguin Books

Chapter Four

'WE CAME INTO THE LAND OF FEAR'

('Nearing the Ancre Battlefield, 1916')

Just before the battalion was ordered to move, Blunden, in his capacity as Field Works Officer, was sent on a course of trench building with the Royal Engineers. The location appealed to him: he was billeted in a beautiful little farmhouse from where he bicycled to Le Plantin, a modest rural hamlet close to Festubert. Then, as now, the ground was water-logged, and Blunden describes groves of willow with old defences running underneath and dugouts scattered with straw. The atmosphere was not one of urgency:

> *our instructor left us here with vague allusion to 'carrying on', and several sappers also went about gravely with hammers and nails. At first we dug with medium force, but the weather was beautiful and even a little too sleepily warm, and presently we withdrew for lunch to one of the ruins behind ...*

Perhaps he was thinking of this episode when he wrote 'Festubert, 1916', published in 1922 when civilian life was difficult; recollecting the more attractive elements of war-time friendship and surroundings in an unhappy post-war time, he sets the scene:

> *Tired with dull grief, grown old before my day,*
> *I sit in solitude and only hear*
> *Long silent laughters, murmurings of dismay,*
> *The lost intensities of hope and fear;*

then takes himself across the familiar landscape behind the lines, with its birds, flowers, trees and supportive atmosphere where he still felt young:

> *There we would go, my friend of friends and I,*
> *And snatch long moments from the grudging wars;*

and in the end:

> *We crept in the tall grass and slept till noon.*

On the second day the participating officers went off for a walk, but on their return they found that the trench they had dug had been spotted by observers in a German kite balloon, and enemy artillery fire had been directed to the site - 'we were offended by the foul smell of recent lyddite, by branches and rafters mutilated and strewn about the crossroad ...' [U/W,p.82]

The course was brief, and Blunden rejoined the battalion. It did not

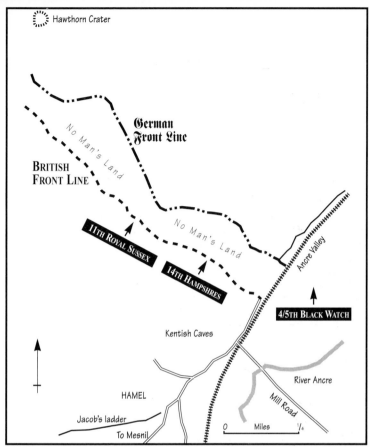

Hawthorn Crater

German Front Line

BRITISH FRONT LINE

No Man's Land

No Man's Land

11TH ROYAL SUSSEX

14TH HAMPSHRES

Ancre Valley

4/5TH BLACK WATCH

Kentish Caves

River Ancre

HAMEL

Mill Road

Jacob's ladder

To Mesnil

0   Miles   ¹/₄

On 3rd September 1916 the 11th Royal Sussex, 14th Hampshres and 4/5th Black Watch went into the attack on the German lines. The attack was not a success. Blunden's duties were with the carrrying parties bringing up ammunition to the front line. Survivors eventually withdrew up Jacob's Ladder or into the Kentish Caves.

move direct to the Somme battlefield, but arrived first, on 14 August 1916, at Monchy Breton, near St. Pol - inevitably known to the troops as Monkey Britain. The terrain was not unlike the section of the Somme battleground that they were destined for, and here they undertook tactical exercises and night attacks, dug dummy trenches and thereafter attacked them. They were instructed on flamethrowers, and Major Campbell, DSO, accompanied by 'well-fed, wool-clad gymnastic demonstrators, preached to us the beauty of the bayonet'. (Earlier in the year Siegfried Sassoon heard the same lecture at the Fourth Army School at Flixécourt, and was both amazed and disgusted by it.)

Although they were not told the name of the village that was to be the object of their attack, they did learn that the jumping-off point was on one side of a valley with the position to be captured on the facing side [U/W, p.86]. With the training period over they moved to Thièvres, south-east of Doullens, where there were disgruntled puns on its name at the villagers' reluctance to provide water for the thirsty troops, except in return for cash payment [U/W p.88].

They moved on to Warnimont Wood, 'an unmolested green cluster' some six or seven miles west of 'the terrible Beaumont Hamel', and officers and NCOs, including Blunden, were sent forward to reconnoitre the new front line on 27 August. The villages that they had known behind the line still harboured civilians, but here in the Somme area all the inhabitants had long since departed. While most of the officers and NCOs went on horseback, Blunden for some reason was mounted on a bicycle - not a happy choice, for the Somme mud did its worst, the brakes locked, and Blunden was thrown off. Reaching Mesnil, under enemy fire, they turned into the western end of a communication trench known as Jacob's Ladder, a dangerous and inhospitable place that lay under continuous enemy observation.

The brief poem *'Escape'* consists of a form of dialogue - *'A Colonel'* states that four officers lay dead in Mesnil, killed by a shell at the foot of Jacob's Ladder, and they must be identified. *'A Mind'* prays that he will not be the one sent *'To view those ravished trunks/And hips and blackened hunks'* and is relieved by *'A Colonel's'* final words: *'No, not you, Bunny, you've just now come down'*. Another officer is sent. Blunden's personal notes indicate that 'Caldwell had the

job, I believe. He had done less than the others, but this must have made up the deficit'.

Jacob's Ladder was a long trench of corners and steep steps that descended through bushes and tall weeds from Mesnil down to Hamel, in the Ancre valley. The trenches ahead were bleak, with ruined houses on the hillsides. Beyond Hamel was 'a small chalk cliff, with a rambling but remarkable dugout in it called Kentish Caves'.

Kentish Caves were named not after Blunden's home county but after the commanding officer of the 1st Battalion East Lancashire Regiment. Early in 1916 Lieutenant-Colonel R. J. Kentish (Royal Irish Fusiliers) instructed the miners in the 1st East Lancs. to construct it, greatly to the benefit of their own unit and many other subsequent users.

Trench names. Most people who consult trench maps must be struck by the variety of names given to them. It is known that familiar names were used for easy identification in

Troops moving through Mesnil which was behind the British front line.

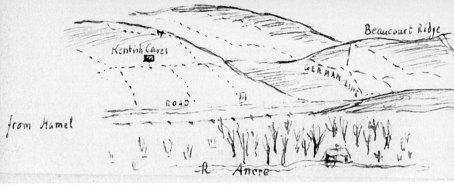

Blunden's sketch of the Kentish Caves

confusing conditions, but some are poetic and almost all are highly evocative.Blunden, as one might expect from someone who enjoyed the uses of language, was intrigued by these names and made notes on various groups of names. His poem 'Trench Nomenclature' celebrates some of them, beginning with *'Jacob's Ladder ran reversed, from earth to a fiery pit extending'*, and continuing via Brock's Benefit (with an appropriate reference to fireworks) and Picturedrome, The Great Wall of China, Krab Krawl, and The Pike and Eel. Handwritten notes in one of his books add more names that caught his imagination - Bond Street, Lover's Lane, Moated Grange and Dormy House - and he noted others that he found interesting: Gunner's Siding, Crow's Nest, White City, Fifth Avenue, Over the Way, Oscar's Copse and Wilde Wood. (These last two were presumably linked in some way.) Some names appeared in many different places, usually well-known London streets, while others were alliterative, musical, or apparently nonsense.

Ruined houses still stood in defiance of the damage they had suffered, grim and menacing in the pastoral setting. One officer whose spirit was not chilled was Lieutenant-Colonel Stanway of the 6th Cheshires - who had taken up his command almost immediately after the Royal Welch's affair at the Red Dragon Crater in June 1916. Evidently a man capable of inspiring effort and confidence, he strode about with what Blunden described as his *'indicatory stick, speaking calmly of the night's shelling, the hard work necessary to keep the trenches open and the enemy's advantage of observation'*. Heartened by Stanway's attitude, Blunden came to regard the Hamel sector as nothing too bad. Colonel Harrison, C.O. of the 11th Royal Sussex, commented to Blunden that Stanway made his men work; Harrison, himself generally at work some twenty hours out of the twenty-four, also commented that the British army was liable to lose the war through not working hard enough.

Lieutenant-Colonel W H Stanway, DSO and Bar, MC

A veteran of the Boer War, Colonel Stanway had been a Company Sergeant Major with the 2nd Bn. Royal Welch Fusiliers in 1914 but by June 1916 held the rank of Captain in that battalion. He was awarded the Military Cross for his action in beating off a German attack at the Duck's Bill Crater (later known as Red Dragon Crater). Shortly afterwards he was promoted to Field rank, taking over command of the 6th Cheshires as a Temporary Lieutenant Colonel. He was wounded on 31 July 1917, during the battle of St. Julien. At the end of the war he served with the South Wales Borderers, with the rank of Captain. He was clearly a brave and distinguished soldier.

As Field Works Officer, Blunden, who was known as 'Rabbit', perhaps because of his restless energy, small neat build and bright alertness (and no doubt also from the easy verbal progression from Blunden to Bunny to Rabbit), had to select positions for the forward dumps of bombs, a vital element for the forthcoming battle. It was here that he met Captain Richard Kirk of the 6th Cheshires, a quiet and reticent man of 31

Lieutenant-Colonel W H Stanway DSO & Bar, MC. South Wales Borderers attached 6th Cheshires. The photograph was taken in 1917. Blunden admired Stanway, and noted his 'indicatory stick' which he is holding here.

from the County Bank, Manchester, (later the NatWest) with lengthy Territorial Force experience. On 1 September 1916 Kirk led a patrol into the German lines and into a dugout, where he shot three German soldiers and then led his patrol back to the British lines without loss.

By now the 11th Royal Sussex were in bivouac in Mailly Wood, ready for the coming attack on 30 August. Wet weather delayed them for a day, and

RICHARD KIRK.
HEAD OFFICE.
Born 7th Feb 1845. Entered the Bank at Stockport 12 Sept 1899. Mobilised 5th Aug 1914. Captain 6th Bn Cheshire Regt
AWARDED THE MILITARY CROSS.
KILLED IN ACTION 13th NOVEMBER 1916 AT BEAUMONT HAMEL, France.

Captain Richard Kirk, MC, 6th Btn Cheshire Regt. County Bank, Manchester, memorial.
NATWEST GROUP ARCHIVES

then another twenty-four hours. By 6.30 pm on 2 September they had relieved the 6th Cheshires in the line and were in their assembly positions ready for a dawn attack on 3 September. As part of the 116th Brigade of the 39th Division, their task was to attack the German lines northwards towards Beaumont Hamel on a front of 1000 yards, together with the 14th Hampshires from the British trenches north of Hamel. The River Ancre lay on their right, with the 4th/5th Black Watch set to work up the Ancre valley and keep in touch with the 49th Division on their right who were attacking in the Thiepval area.

At first the attack by the Sussex and Hampshire men on the morning of 3 September was successful, with both battalions securing the German front line trenches against very little opposition; any resistance was eliminated by the British machine guns firing over their heads. The Hampshires lost heavily and barely advanced thereafter, while the 11th Royal Sussex did better and drove the Germans from parts of the support trench, some individuals actually reaching the trenches beyond.

In the Ancre valley, meanwhile, the Black Watch suffered severely from machine-gun fire and made very little progress. To their right, the troops of the 49th Division were driven back:

> Thiepval is not yet captured: and we have heard that on September the Third the 49th Division could not get twenty yards forward from Thiepval Wood - Oh, forget September the Third. We are still in the Somme battle, and probably only just beginning. [U/W, p.103]

The struggle became a battle between opposing bombers, each party being up to forty strong. Despite advance planning and strategically placed ammunition dumps, the supply of British bombs was exhausted and eventually, with little progress achieved, the Corps Commander withheld the reserves and brought the Ancre operation of 3 September to a halt. Survivors of the 11th Royal Sussex attack, trapped in No Man's Land in shell-holes and other places, had to wait until nightfall before they could return to their own lines.

The two men who had been placed under open arrest for apparently condoning fraternisation with the enemy were both in action. Second Lieutenant Cassels rallied his men from a moment of disorganisation, while Redway was wounded. Other friends of Blunden's were involved in the day's activities: Doogan, who joined the battalion at the same time, was wounded, and Captain Northcote held on in a precarious position but was killed as he returned in the early evening after being forced out of the German second lines. His body was never found, and

Into the trenches at Beaucourt, in the Ancre Valley. IWM Q 4522

his name is recorded on the panels of the Thiepval Memorial. Captain Penruddocke, another friend and formerly Blunden's Company Commander, was also killed; he is buried in Serre Road No. 2 cemetery.

Another casualty was Second Lieutenant Charles Vorley who had trained in England with Blunden and who showed him how to post sentries and set off flares at Festubert. Badly wounded during his platoon's attack, Vorley was taken prisoner and died ten days later. He is buried in Caudry Old Communal cemetery near Le Cateau, used by the Germans as a cemetery for Allied prisoners and constructed by them with forced French labour.

It was a sad day; by 5.30 pm the battalion had lost some 300 men killed, wounded and missing. Relieved by Lieutenant-Colonel Stanway and the 6th Cheshires, the 11th Royal Sussex went into billets at Englebelmer.

Blunden, in charge of carrying parties, did not take part in the actual assault. Amidst the roaring explosions and scurrying messengers the subdued and nervous carriers waited and smoked, sitting in their cellar, while he led groups with their bomb buckets out into the heat of the battle. Their route to the front lines led along the Hamel road, which ran beside the railway line and the River Ancre. Here they met bedraggled wounded of the Black Watch trailing down the road to the sand-bagged dressing station after wading up the river in their attempt

67

to capture a German machine-gun post. The German line a few yards ahead was invisible in mist and smoke as Blunden directed the delivery and returned to Kentish Caves.

Undertones of War [pp. 97-101] gives a powerful description of the strain, the noise and the confusion of the day:

> *The British barrage struck. The air gushed in hot surges along that river valley, and uproar never imagined by me swung from ridge to ridge. The east was scarlet with dawn and the flickering gunflashes; I thanked God I was not in the assault, and joined the subdued carriers nervously lighting cigarettes in one of the cellars, sitting there on the steps, studying my watch. The ruins of Hamel were soon crashing chaotically with German shells, and jags of iron and broken wood and brick whizzed past the cellar mouth. When I gave the word to move, it was obeyed with no pretence of enthusiasm. I was forced to shout and swear, and the carrying party, some with shoulders hunched, as if in a snowstorm, dully picked up their bomb buckets and went ahead.*
>
> *The wreckage around seemed leaping with flame.* [U/W, pp.97-8]

He describes himself as inarticulate and others as 'staring like persons in a trance across No Man's Land, their powers of action apparently suspended', and the overcrowded atmosphere of Kentish Caves one of 'ominous discommunication'. The frantic conditions, Colonel Harrison 'with a face all doubt and stress', the efforts to send messages, the deadlock, the alarm at a rumour (unfounded) that there were Germans in the British front line trench - which threatened to make Kentish Caves a death-trap - and the burst of activity that this provoked in the heavy mid-day heat, are all presented.

The bombers were running short of ammunition and 'Rabbit' was summoned to set out with fresh supplies – but the order was cancelled, to keep all available men ready for defence against the expected attack. It proved to be a false alarm.

L/Sergeant H. Davey (k.i.a 9.8.16) (left) and Sergeant Frank Worley.

Above all, Blunden describes the confusion of the day, the over-complication of the plans of manoeuvre, and the 'singular fact that no one .. could say what had happened, or what was happening'. Wounded runners appeared with messages from time to time, as did Sergeant Unstead, a former companion of Blunden at Festubert, his normal equanimity now disturbed. Wounded men from the battalion and some from the Black Watch sought shelter in the caves, but unfortunately the Germans had got the range of the shelter and caused casualties when they hit the entrance. One of these was No. SD/429 Sergeant F. A. Hoad, from Eastbourne. His wound was slight - a mere scratch from a splinter - but he refused to believe that it was genuinely a minor injury. Neither the encouragement of Blunden's Sergeant Worley nor a tot of rum could overcome the shock, and Hoad died; Blunden describes the incident in his poem 'Pillbox', in which he describes the sergeant as 'A good man, Hoad, for weeks' and 'out burst terrors that he'd striven to tame'.

This sensitive description of a man overcome with strain and shock, his everyday self-control defeated, is typical of Blunden's close observation and ability to express death and high drama in quiet and conversational tones, underlining the combination of hard physical effort, danger and sudden violent death [U/W, p.260].

As the survivors returned it was apparent that no one, not even those who had been in the attack, could say what had taken place. The German defences with their intricate series of tunnels had enabled the enemy to come up behind the backs of the Royal Sussex. Orders for the battalion to withdraw were sent out by runners; some survived and enabled the remnants of the battalion to reassemble, and as they wound their way to safety, the enemy added to their problems in the darkness and the battletorn landscape by raining down gas shells on them.

Although Blunden characteristically plays it down, it may well have been his share in the day's activities that earned him the recommendation for the Military Cross (see below, page 95).

The Royal Sussex withdrew to billets in Englebelmer, though even here they were not entirely safe. The turf in the orchard outside the billet was gouged out by heavy shells, as high explosive splintered the heavily-laden apple trees and the comfortable village houses. The Germans had found their range, and the battalion was shelled at intervals round the clock. During this turbulent 'rest' time the battalion reorganised itself after the heavy casualties of 3 September: the remnants of the four companies were formed into two, with A and D forming No. 1 and D and C forming No. 2, under the command of

Second Lieutenant Cassels with Blunden assisting. Hitherto the 11th Royal Sussex had maintained a semblance of its original self but now, like the many battalions ('Pals' and others) which had suffered so severely in the Battle of the Somme, it was to change considerably in its composition.

On 6 September they moved into billets in Beaussart, which had not been shelled and still housed 'some sulky civilians'. Here they were joined by nearly 500 reinforcements, only 70 of them men from the Royal Sussex Regiment and the remainder from no fewer than eleven battalions of other regiments, including some from Cyclist units. When Blunden collected one of the drafts from the railhead at Belle Eglise, he observed the triumphant march to the billet, but recognised that the men knew why they were there. In Beaussart, the troops watched Colincamps burning under a bombardment of heavy shells.

Ten days later the 11th Royal Sussex was back in the front line in the Beaumont sector after relieving their sister battalion, the 12th Royal Sussex. In Undertones of War Blunden sought to emphasise the tranquillity of this period, but he has to admit to 'ungentle interludes' [U/W, p.107]. These included enemy artillery and trench mortar barrages, resulting in a steady stream of casualties within the battalion. Unusually, two Other Ranks who were wounded on 18 September were designated as suffering from 'shell shock' - a description more often seen later in the war, and in any case more often encountered in diagnosing officers. Gas shells falling on the lines on 23 September were an unwelcome baptism for the new draft of 125 men who had arrived from the comparative quiet of Mailly-Maillet a few days earlier.

Although a German raid anticipated by the Colonel had Blunden and his fellow second lieutenant, Cassels, waiting for most of one night with carefully selected soldiers and bombs at the ready for an assault that never happened, on 20 September enemy fire smashed into a dugout and Blunden saw the terribly mangled bodies of the already-dead victims of an earlier bombardment [U/W, p.107-8]. The battalion continued to suffer German shellings of varying intensity, mostly connected to the forthcoming British attack on Thiepval. The village was still in German hands on 25 September 1916 - but not for much longer.

Before 1914 Thiepval was a quiet village with its church, barns and snug cottages standing at a height of about 500 feet and dominating the rolling farmland around it. On 1 July 1916 the 15th and 16th Lancashire Fusiliers (1st and 2nd Salford Pals) failed to capture this prominent objective despite very heavy casualties. In spite of continued efforts to take the village, now a mass of churned-up earth, tree stumps, shell craters and ruined buildings, the British troops met with no success here. On the night of 26-27 September, however, the 18th Division under Major-General Ivor Maxse undertook a fresh attack, and with a combination of determination and well-thought-out methods the British finally captured and occupied Thiepval.

The 11th Royal Sussex played a small part in capturing the site, by diverting some of the German artillery fire away from the attacking troops on the right of the battalion. Their method was to prepare 190 dummies, padded out with grass and sandbags, and set them on the parapet to look like troops going over, with a smoke barrage to add confusion. The deceit was highly effective, bringing shrapnel fire down onto the Royal Sussex front line and supports and away from the genuine attacking forces.

The battalion remained in the front line trenches until it was relieved by the 14th Battalion Hampshire Regiment on 4 October - three weeks, an unusually long stay, as Blunden remarked. He also noted General Hornby's cryptic phrasing to tell Colonel Harrison of the impending relief: 'You will have your tea this evening, Harrison ...' - 'tea' being the General's code for trench relief [U/W, p.112]

Blunden, meanwhile, was occupied with his field works, and in the

Royal Engineers' HQ, October 1916, The White House in Mailly-Maillet. Blunden was deeply impressed by this house when he visited the Engineers' dump nearby.

The Ancre Valley, looking north and showing the war damaged tree-stumps. IWM Q 1545

course of his duties came across a 'large forgotten wealth' of carpenter's stores, ranging from axes to heavy baulks of timber. He directed his men to bring in some of this material, and took part in the work at one stage; the morning mist lifted suddenly, revealing him and his men between the British front and support lines to any interested enemy observer. He was clearly not averse to youthful risks, as when he and his friend Second Lieutenant Cassels spent a happy hour tossing Mills bombs from a trench catapult across a great crater in front of the German line, where they burst like shrapnel [U/W, p.110].

He moved around the area behind the lines, and on one occasion walked to Mailly-Maillet to gather material from the Royal Engineers' dump. Beside it he explored the house of a local notary, with his books stacked throughout the house and covered in powdered glass and plaster. He picked up a few volumes to take back to his trench in a sandbag. Such finds were a reassurance in the surroundings of war. The Royal Engineers' HQ was an impressive building, white-painted and elegantly furnished - even the sandbags protecting the windows had been painted white, a striking touch in the war-ravaged landscape.

This was not the only time Blunden had a happy find: billetted in Arras after the Armistice, in the semi-ruined fabric of a battered house he found a copy of Edward Thomas's study of John Keats - and, knowing that Thomas, whose life and work he much admired, had been based in Arras at the time of his death in 1917, hoped that it might perhaps have been the poet's own copy.

When the battalion was relieved it marched off to Martinsart Wood, full of howitzers, mud and huts; but the eye of the poet appreciated the woodland wilderness of some undisturbed thickets.

On 5 October 1916 the battalion was placed under the orders of the 117th Brigade. Changes were expected. Next day Blunden was one of a group of 'unlucky officers' sent to reconnoitre Thiepval Wood. Under heavy fire they made their way to a dugout which Blunden referred to

as Gordon House, probably Gordon Castle - stout-looking, but generally agreed to provide inadequate protection. Colonel Harrison instructed Blunden on bombing blocks. (Blocks interrupting the line of trenches, to prevent enemy attacks bombing up the trench.) The group discovered that they would not after all be involved in the forthcoming attack on Thiepval Wood, but were to be part of the 116th Brigade once again. They returned to Hamel, back across the river to the exposed flanks of Jacob's Ladder which faced the threatening ridge of Thiepval.

Writing *Undertones of War* more than a decade later, far away in Japan and without reference material, Blunden recalled this river valley, the villages and woods of the Ancre, with great clarity, and a kind of solemn affection - for the atmosphere, the scenery, or for his own youthful self? He was very conscious of the ordinary domesticity of the original landscape, the railway line running down to Albert where surely the regular train would appear at any moment, and the woodland tracks through the surviving trees. The watery valley-bottom, the sights and scents of damp woodland in its autumn colours, were a powerful reminder of his childhood and drew him back into the pre-war delight in matching language to his close observation of nature.

On 7 October Colonel Harrison set out to reconnoitre the new lines at Hamel, and by noon that day the battalion was back in the front line. It was quiet - but three soldiers were wounded and two members of the Lewis gun course were killed on fatigue duty. The trickle of casualties continued as the battalion prepared to cooperate in the Brigade's attack on the Schwaben Redoubt.

On 9 October the 16th Sherwood Foresters made a surprise attack on the Schwaben Redoubt - initially successful, but then repulsed. Other battalions took over, with dramatically effective results and by 14 October the 4/5th Black Watch and 6th Cheshires, both like the 11th Royal Sussex members of the 39th Division, had attacked and completed the final capture of the Redoubt. The role of the 11th Royal Sussex was to discharge smoke canisters, in order to divert enemy fire,

73

Troops sorting out rations and supplies. These soldiers are wearing jerkins over their uniforms, which were issued as the weather grew colder.

and to keep the Germans under heavy machine-gun and sniper fire.

The battalion rested in Authuille Wood, and prepared for the forthcoming attack, on 21 October - part of the battle for the Ancre Heights. Blunden, who seemed to have a knack for discovering supplies of stores and rations, came across a half-collapsed cellar full of Army rations. First the battalion took its fill of marmalades, soups and other items, and then the discovery was reported to Brigade HQ and thousands of tins of food were sent down to them. He pondered on the men, working in 'the exact and ordinary manner of the British working man', and wondered who they were, what their thoughts might be. He thought of them as willing, shy, thinking of their families; but 'almost all were to finish their peaceful lives in the fury of Stuff trench'. [U/W, p.117]. On 20 October they relieved their sister battalion in the line.

The Battle of the Ancre Heights was to continue with various breaks until 11 November 1916. Blunden and his friend Second Lieutenant Cassels MC went forward to the battalion's start line, to make a dump of tools, ammunition and other materials ready for the attack. Their walk took them to the front line 'over the most bewildering battlefield so gouged and hummocked, so denatured and dun, so crowded with brown shrapnel cases and German long-handled grenades, shell holes, rifles' that it was 'a billowing desert'. A German aircraft flying thirty yards above their trench fired on them, but fortunately missed its aim.

Blunden's 39th Division was to attack to the west and east of the Schwaben Redoubt, part of an enormous attack on the heights by four divisions along a front of some 4500-5000 yards. Within this plan, the task of the 11th Royal Sussex was to take the formidable Stuff Trench, which ran north-east from the northern tip of the Schwaben Redoubt, crossing the Thiepval-Grandcourt road and connecting with Regina trench which ran due west. The trench was duly taken - but at a very heavy cost.

The battalion's War Diary for 21 October is brief, only five lines, and states modestly:

> *The battalion capture German First line (Stuff Trench). Heavy casualties were inflicted upon the enemy and many prisoners taken.*

The entry records eleven O.R.s killed, 186 wounded and 77 missing.

The attack on Stuff Trench. Stuff Trench was captured on 21 October 1916 by the 116th Brigade. this included the 11th Royal Sussex, whose casualties here numbered 274.

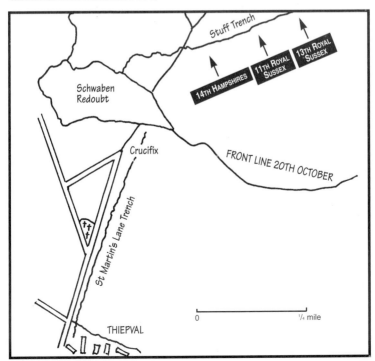

Panorama of the Ancre Valley, looking towards the Schwaben Redoubt.
IWM Q1545

Also among the killed was Second Lieutenant William Doogan, who was with Blunden when they joined the battalion at Festubert on 14 May. He had had some premonition about his death. Just before the attack he had said, 'It's the third time they've sent me over. This is the third time. They'll get me this time.' He was wounded, after the capture of Stuff Trench, and was then killed by a shell landing in one of the dug-out shafts. His body was never found: he is commemorated on the panels of the Thiepval Memorial, just a few hundred yards away from the location of his death with so many thousands of others.

Blunden was ordered to take A and D companies over to reinforce the men holding the recently captured Stuff Trench. Here he found that his friend Second Lieutenant Geoffrey Salter had just buried his own brother Francis, serving with him in B company and killed in the hail of shells falling around them. Francis Salter's body was eventually moved to Mill Road cemetery, not far from where his brother had buried him.

The survivors were relieved next day, and marched to bivouacs in Aveluy Wood back across the river. Next, stretcher bearers searched the captured trenches for the many wounded men, and brought them back to the field ambulance. As Blunden noted, this action in Stuff Trench on 21-22 October was the first in which the battalion had captured and held any of the German area, and the cost was very severe: and there was no hope that the Somme battle might be over. [U/W, pp.122-126].

Winter clothing was issued as the weather grew colder, and on 29 October every available officer and man in the battalion (13 officers, 390 Other Ranks) marched to Thiepval Wood to work on a new reserve trench line, and next day they took over 'that deathtrap known as the Schwaben Redoubt.' It was a move that placed them in an 'almost obliterated cocoon of trenches in which mud and death were much the same thing' with deep dugouts facing the German lines 'cancerous with torn bodies and to pass an entrance was to gulp poison'. (Blunden's fellow-feeling for the poetry of Wilfred Owen, clearly visible in the long memoir that he wrote to his edition of Owen's poetry for publication in 1931, can surely be seen in these descriptions).

Near the 11th Royal Sussex position men holding the line were found up to their armpits in thick mud, drowning in the thick viscous

76

ooze from which it was impossible to retrieve them. 'Their fate was not spoken of ... those that found them could not get them out'; the whole zone, in Blunden's words, was 'a corpse and the mud itself was mortified'.

Colonel Harrison had set up battalion headquarters in a deep former German dugout at the Thiepval end of the St. Martin's Lane communication trench, running north from the crossroads in what had once been Thiepval and almost parallel with the line of the modern road. Intense shelling had turned it into a wide morass, nearly full of thick mud. [U/W, p.130]. The journey from the headquarters to the line was a terrible one, which would take even an experienced runner four or five hours for the round trip: in 1929 Blunden met one of the runners, H. T. Norman, who confirmed this. The battalion's reserve company was based in a captured German dugout in Thiepval, deep enough to have two storeys. Inquiring as ever, Blunden discovered a dark gallery below the lower level, where he found stacks of high explosive originally intended for use in blowing a mine to destroy the earlier British line by the Ancre. Further stores included smart new German greatcoats and tins of meat with Russian labels, which proved unpopular with the British troops.

'Premature Rejoicing' is one of the ways in which Blunden dealt with his experiences around Thiepval. Opening *'What's that over there? Thiepval Wood./Take a steady look at it; it'll do you good'* the poem speaks of Titania, the Fairy Queen, smiling through her tears and looking ten years ahead to see the wood in good health again; distancing himself from the

Stuff Trench, modern view taken from the site of the German lines in October 1916 looking towards the British front lines at Thiepval, (which lies just beyond the horizon). The Grandcourt-Thiepval road runs between the hedges at the centre, with Grandcourt behind the camera. Stuff Trench can be located today by the line of tall trees on the horizon to the left of the picture, while the similar tall trees at the far right are on the site of the Hansa Line. It was somewhere between the camera and the Hansa Line that Blunden and his runner first realised that they were lost, during a reconnaissance.

Mill Road, 1916 and 1998: A water-filling point on Mill Road where it crosses the River Ancre. Troops filling empty petrol cans with water from the river, with three horsemen riding along Mill Road towards Thiepval Wood. In later years, the troops have gone and the trees have grown, but the river flows on. IWM Q4579

present 'din', he ends delicately and matter-of-factly:

> *... it's a shade too soon*
> *For you to scribble rhymes*
> *In your army book*
> *About those times;*
> *Take another look;*
> *That's where the difficulty is, over there.*

It was here, and on this date, that Blunden took over the daily task of writing up the battalion diary. The encouraging review of his poems that Colonel Harrison had spotted in the *Times Literary Supplement* in June may have inspired this appointment. Reading his contributions to the battalion's history, it is immediately apparent (even without the initials 'EB' in the diary Remarks Column), that a discerning writer has temporarily taken over the daily record. Praise is given where appropriate, concerning both individuals and the battalion as a whole. The choice of language and style of writing, together with the increased length of the entries, are immediately striking, and indicate a writer who enjoys using his skills with the written word.

There was even an opportunity to make a tactful military point while appearing helpful. In the past Blunden had commented on the army's sometimes wasteful practice of sending an excessive number of men to carry out simple tasks; the War Diary for 7 November, when the battalion was on rest, records the instructions that every available

The Ancre Battlefield 1916. A sketch map showing the location of the Schwaben Redoubt, Stuff Trench and the St Martin's Lane communication trench. These places were very familiar to Blunden and the 11th Royal Sussex in October-November 1916.

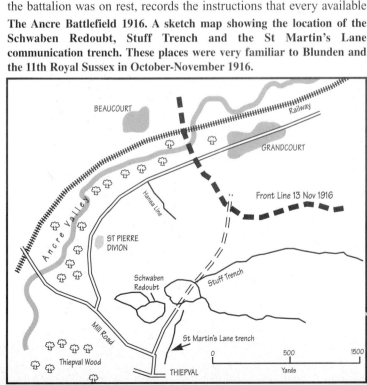

man was to be employed on a working party in Aveluy and Nab Valley, and when Blunden wrote up the day's diary he records that the tasks could have been done better by about 120 men. It is not known whether any notice was taken of this opinion!

Colonel Harrison habitually carried a letter of resignation, available to be handed to his General if some desperate order was received. One such occasion occurred during a visit from the Brigadier-General - Harrison handed over his letter to the senior officer, who declined to look at it and put it in his breeches pocket. The Colonel finally gained his point, and also an entertaining personal anecdote.

The Royal Sussex had an uncomfortable change of quarters as they were being relieved by the 6th Cheshires on 1 November, for the movement was noticed by the enemy and both battalions suffered casualties from heavy shelling. During this brief period out of the line a group of officers was ordered to visit Toutencourt, some dozen miles away. The purpose was to view a new patent oven, constructed from five oil drums, being displayed by 'a selection of Staff Officers', after which Blunden lorry-hopped back from 'aristocratic Toutencourt ... to democratic Thiepval'. He was informed of the approaching major attack, General Gough's decision to launch his offensive on 13 November 1916.

Contrasts behind the line: 'At Senlis Once' In his oblique way, Blunden emphasises the dangers and discomforts of war conditions by delighting in a peaceful village behind the lines, seen during one of their rest periods:

O how comely it was and how reviving
When with clay and with death no longer striving
Down firm roads we came to houses
With women chattering and green grass thriving.

He depicts the pleasure of living in this quiet present, regardless of the next spell in the front line and celebrates the sturdy attitudes of his soldiers, enjoying a visiting pierrot show 'with lusty laughter':

Even could ridicule their own sufferings,
Sang as though nothing but joy came after!

The Grandcourt-Thiepval road as it approaches Thiepval – the British memorial is visible, top centre. St Martin's Lane communication trench ran parallel to the road in the field on the left of the photograph. Thiepval cemetery is behind the camera, with its access footpath leading to the area of the Schwaben Redoubt and the front-line trenches located behind and to the right of the camera.

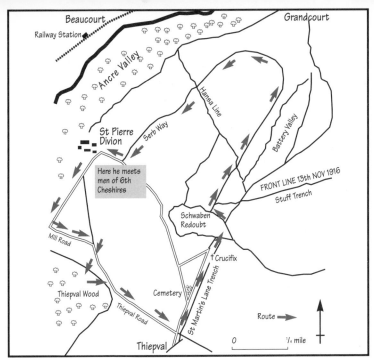

The map labels include:

Beaucourt · Grandcourt · Railway Station · Ancre Valley · Hansa Line · Battery Valley · St Pierre Divion · Serb Way · Here he meets men of 6th Cheshires · FRONT LINE 13th NOV 1916 · Stuff Trench · Schwaben Redoubt · Mill Road · † Crucifix · St Martin's Lane Trench · Thiepval Wood · Cemetery · Thiepval Road · Route ➝ · Thiepval · 0 · ¼ mile

A Lively Journey – Blunden gets lost on a reconnaissance in advance of the positions recently captured by the Royal Naval Division. The arrowed line indicates his route, when he and his runner, as he wrote in the battalion War Diary, 'overshot their mark, almost reaching Grandcourt'.

Back in the Schwaben Redoubt again, Blunden was nearly placed in command of a bombing raid against a German strong-point some forty yards in front of the British lines. In the event his friend Lieutenant Cassels was sent instead, during the evening of 11 November. Cassels and his sergeant were under bombardment and fusillades, until fortunately two of the enemy appeared from a different direction and surrendered, one a milkman and one a schoolmaster. The incident was

The Ancre Battlefield/ the Schwaben Redoubt. Taken from the heights above the River Ancre (which is hidden in the trees nearest the camera). When Blunden lost his way after leaving the Schwaben Redoubt he eventually returned via the Hansa Line (top left). St Pierre Divion, then recently captured, lies in the trees to the left of the picture. Leaving St Pierre Divion, Blunden followed the banks of the river to Thiepval Wood via Mill Road, which leads up from the valley and past the Ulster Tower.

glowingly written up in the war diary by a grateful Blunden, who made the retrieval of the prisoners much more of an active exploit on Cassels' part. Cassels' contention that the enemy post was too firmly held for assault was readily accepted at Brigade HQ.

The final offensive of the Somme battle, which was to consist of five days of intense fighting, began on the morning of 13 November 1916, with the 39th Division - including the 11th Royal Sussex - heavily involved. The Division was instructed to clear the Germans from the slope above the River Ancre as far to the north-east as the Hansa Line, which extended down to the river valley near St. Pierre Divion and opposite the edge of Beaucourt.

Responsibility for this part of the clearance was allocated to the 6th Cheshires under Colonel Stanway, who were in the line to the left of the 11th Royal Sussex. The Cheshires' attack began at 5.45 am, with the objective of capturing St. Pierre Division on the east bank of the River Ancre; by noon it was in British hands and all the Cheshires' objectives were secure. One of the earliest casualties was Captain Kirk, killed at around 6 am.

Orders came through at 4.00 pm that day for the 11th Royal Sussex to provide 300 men and some officers, under Captain Cooling (the battalion's second in command), to carry coils of wire and wire pickets to a particular trench map reference, as part of the consolidation of the day's gains. From the War Diary this spot can be located as lying close to the present-day Ulster Tower. Reconnaissance was essential, immediately, and Blunden was detailed for the task with Private Johnson, his runner.

By the time they set off it was almost dark, and the mist quickly changed to drizzle.

> *...we set off at once, seeing that there was a heavy barrage*

Metal Harvest 1998: ammunition ploughed up in the fields near Beaumont Hamel.

eastward, but knowing that it was best not to think about it. What light the grudging day had permitted was now almost extinct, and the mist had changed into a drizzle; we passed...the scrawled Schwaben - few people about, white lights whirling up north of the Ancre, and the shouldering hills north and east gathering inimical mass in their wan illusion. Crossing scarcely discernible remains of redoubts and communications, I saw an officer peering from a little furrow of trench ahead, and went to him. 'Is this our front line?' 'Dunno: you get down off there, you'll be hit.'... I said to Johnson, 'the front line must be ahead here still; come on.' We were now in the dark and, before we realised it, inside a barrage; never had shells seemed so torrentially swift, so murderous. [U/W, pp.137-8]*

They passed the crucifix on the Thiepval - Grandcourt road, and the

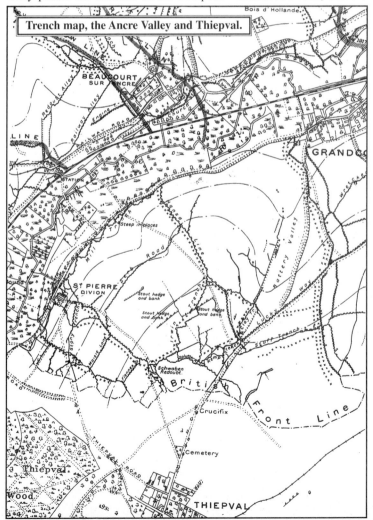

Trench map, the Ancre Valley and Thiepval.

Schwaben Redoubt - and then realised that they were lost. They pressed on, none the less, at one moment amongst abandoned German howitzer positions with dead men in grey overcoats at dugout entrances. A Maxim gun opened fire on them - but suddenly Blunden saw the distant lagoons of the River Ancre shimmering in the lights of Beaucourt. He knew now where he was, and the two men ran and plunged, half-crouching through the cascading shells, until they were challenged in English - they were back in the British front line near St. Pierre Divion, astonishingly alive after their 'accidental tour into enemy country' [U/W, p.138].

The way back to Thiepval was easier, and soon the nimble young officer and his 'white-faced' runner were back in battalion HQ where they were greeted 'as Lazarus was' - their certain deaths had been assumed. Colonel Harrison was on the telephone to Brigadier-General Hornby as the two men entered battalion HQ and told him at once 'that these are men who have been through terrific shelling': the wiring party was immediately cancelled on the strength of Blunden's report, and Captain Cooling and his men were given new orders.

Blunden's last task for the day was to write up the War Diary. Neatly, modestly and impersonally, he wrote briefly of his experiences for Monday 13 November 1916:

> *At 4 pm orders came through for 300 men and a proportion of officers under Captain Cooling to carry coils of wire to [trench map reference given], and a patrol of 1 officer and runner were immediately sent up to find the best way. They had a lively journey and overshot their mark, almost reaching Grandcourt. Eventually returning via HANSA LINE, SERB WAY, ST. PIERRE DIVION, MILL ROAD and THIEPVAL WOOD, they reported a heavy barrage behind Schwaben and a worse on the HANSA LINE. The orders were then modified and the party carried the wire up to the Schwaben Redoubt.*

There is no hint of the two men's extraordinary escape from almost overwhelming danger.

There was, indeed, no time to brood over it, for the battalion moved out the same evening into a hutted camp behind the lines, and two days later the battalion was on the march again, on their way out of the Somme sector and north to Ypres.

Visit. Leave Thiepval on the D 151 road towards Grandcourt, stopping at the village cemetery a short way along on the left of the road, beside the path leading off to the left.

Leave the car by the road-side, and follow the path as it leads across the hillside and down towards the Ancre valley and St. Pierre Divion. From the point at which the track begins to dip down towards the river and St. Pierre Divion it is possible to appreciate the scale of the task that the British troops undertook in order to capture the Schwaben Redoubt and the surrounding battlefield.

In addition, there is a magnificent view across the Ancre Valley, taking in Hamel, Newfoundland Park, and the western flanks of the Ancre valley, the scene of the abortive dawn attack by Blunden's battalion on 3 September 1916.

Return to the car and drive on towards Grandcourt. Shortly beyond the large farm on the crest of the hill, the long line of trees stretching up to the right marks the approximate site of Stuff Trench, the capture of which on 21 October 1916 cost Blunden's battalion so much.

At Grandcourt, turn left on to the D 163 E, leading through St. Pierre Divion (captured by the 6th Cheshires on 13 November 1916) to the T-junction with Mill Road. Turn right, go over the railway level crossing and turn right immediately beyond it on to the D 50. After passing the Ancre Cemetery on the left, turn left in Beaucourt-sur-Ancre on to the D 163, leading towards Beaumont Hamel. Here again there are good views of the 1916 battlefields which emphasise once again the challenge that the British troops had to undertake to capture these heights.

Leave Beaumont Hamel heading north on the D 163. As it runs up

Old German front line near Beaumont Hamel. TAYLOR LIBRARY

the shallow valley, look to the high bank on the left: the clump of trees on the ridge marks the famous Hawthorn Mine Crater (the explosion of this mine on 1 July 1916 was filmed by Geoffrey Malins, one of the best-known and frequently shown film clips of the Battle of Somme). On the right of the road, the CWGC cemetery is set on part of the site of the disastrous attack by the Lancashire Fusiliers on 1 July 1916.

Continue up the D 163 to Auchonvillers and turn left. Newfoundland Park, the great memorial park to the men of Newfoundland who fell here on 1 July 1916, lies on the left of the road as you head back towards the Ancre valley. The road drops down steeply into the valley, offering magnificent views of the battlefield across the valley immediately ahead. Even today, depending on the time of year and state of the fields, it is possible to follow the line of the trenches by streaks of chalk sub-soil brought to the surface on the hillside. At the bottom, turn right to see the CWGC cemetery at Hamel - 'open all hours' as Blunden describes it - close by.

Reverse direction and drive north along the valley road. Just before the turning right to head back across the level crossing towards Thiepval, look to the left of the road: a low escarpment beyond the field next to the road is the probable site of the large dug-out system known as Kentish Caves.

Across the railway line and river, the Ulster Tower stands near the crest of the hill with two CWGC cemeteries near it: Connaught, on the right of the road, and Mill Road on the left. The latter, accessible up a narrow grass path, is unusual in having many of its headstones laid horizontally because of the instability of the ground - the result of old dugouts collapsing beneath it. The view looking north from Mill Road cemetery gives another view of the Schwaben Redoubt area.

Return to the car and drive into Thiepval village to complete the circuit of this part of the Somme and Ancre battlefield

The Kentish Caves, view from Ulster Tower. Blunden was here in September 1916. The River Ancre runs across the view, below the site of the entrance to the Caves, with Newfoundland Park on the horizon.

KENTISH CAVES

Chapter Five

THE SALIENT

'Why, see old Stevens there, that iron man,
Melting the ice to shave his grotesque chin!'
· · · · · · · ·
'Watch as you will, men clench their chattering teeth
And freeze you back with that one hope, disdain.'
from 'The Zonnebeke Road', *Undertones of War*

On 18 November 1916, the official final day of the Battle of the Somme, the 11th Royal Sussex arrived at Poperinghe long before dawn in bitterly cold weather. Among the names selected for promotion or award at this time was Blunden's friend Second Lieutenant Geoffrey Salter, who had buried his brother the previous month on the battlefield near Stuff Trench. Salter received the Military Cross and was promoted to command one of the battalion's companies, with the rank of Captain.

The Menin Gate, 1999.

It was the town of Ypres, more than any other single location, which illustrated the static nature of most of the First World War, for its defence involved four main operations over a period of four years. In the breathless turmoil of 1914, the First Battle of Ypres lasted for just over four weeks (October-November). 'Second Ypres', 22 April - 25 May 1915, included battles at Gravenstafel Ridge, where the Canadians were involved in the German gas attack, and at St. Julien. 'Third Ypres' began with the Battle of Pilckem on 31 July 1917 and culminated with the end of the Second Battle of Passchendaele on 10 November, while the defence of Ypres in April 1918 was part of the final successful series of operations which led to the Armistice. The desperate and unending struggle to

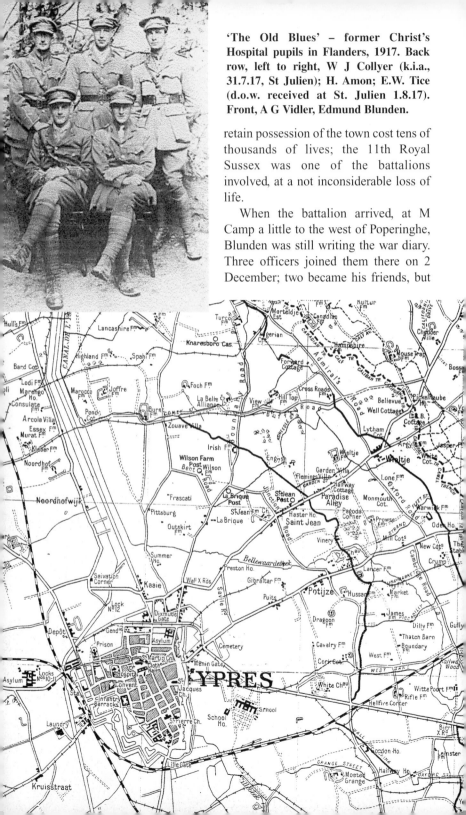

'The Old Blues' – former Christ's Hospital pupils in Flanders, 1917. Back row, left to right, W J Collyer (k.i.a., 31.7.17, St Julien); H. Amon; E.W. Tice (d.o.w. received at St. Julien 1.8.17). Front, A G Vidler, Edmund Blunden.

retain possession of the town cost tens of thousands of lives; the 11th Royal Sussex was one of the battalions involved, at a not inconsiderable loss of life.

When the battalion arrived, at M Camp a little to the west of Poperinghe, Blunden was still writing the war diary. Three officers joined them there on 2 December; two became his friends, but the third met with less approval - this was Captain Owen, who took command of the battalion when Colonel Harrison went on leave on 5 December. The arriving draft included two Second Lieutenants, Vidler (an 'Old Blue') and Whitley, 'soon styled O.C. Daily Mirror' [U/W p.148]. Another 'Old Blue', Second Lieutenant Amon, had joined the battalion the previous month.

Arnold Vidler was born in British Columbia, and returned to Canada after leaving Christ's Hospital. At the outbreak of war he immediately joined the Canadian cavalry, and arrived in France early in 1915 as a trooper in Lord Strathcona's Horse. In May 1915 he was severely wounded in the head by shrapnel while consolidating a captured German trench near Festubert. Later he was commissioned in the Royal Sussex, but after returning to the front too soon he had to return to England. In all he had a distinguished miitary career, and survived the war. Blunden describes him as 'that invincible soldier'. Sadly, his wounds - from which he never fully recovered - and the loss of his only brother near Arras in 1917 led to severe mental distress. In 1924 he took his own life, and Blunden's poem 'A.G.A.V.' is a touching elegy in honour of his friend [U/W p.268].

After a brief training period at Moulle, near St. Omer, a lucky few left for ten days' leave in England. Blunden returned to Poperinghe on Christmas Eve 1916, where he was put in charge of a draft of

British officers in St Omer market, 1918 (IWM Q.11074)

German trench at Ypres. Note the grave on the right of the photograph.

reinforcements destined for the 11th Royal Sussex and moved up to the front line. During his leave the battalion had been ordered to relieve the 1st Battalion Hertfordshire Regiment at Essex Farm on the Yser canal bank north of the town. At this time the Ypres Salient was one of the quietest sectors of the Western Front, and units that had suffered in the Somme fighting were sent there for a less testing period.

Lieutenant-Colonel Harrison, the Commanding Officer, also rejoined the battalion on Christmas Eve 1916. Blunden reported on the

Christmas Day service conducted by the colonel next day; apparently as the C.O. was reading the Lesson the regimental band mistook its cue and 'thundered out "While Shepherds Watched"' while the reading was still in progress. The C.O. had another challenge to undertake that day - in accordance with tradition he and his second in command and adjutant visited each company at dinner, and with each one had to drink down a mug of a specially concocted drink to celebrate the day. 'Rest and celebrations' continued on Boxing Day [U/W, p.152].

By New Year's Eve there were parties of a different kind, in No

Man's Land in the front line north of Ypres at Boesinghe, where they had taken over the line from the 10th South Wales Borderers. South of the devastated village of Boesinghe, and just north of the point where the railway line crossed the Yser canal, a burned-out château stood close to the canal on its western bank. Battalion headquarters here 'was an iron vault in an outbuilding, with fragile huts and coop-like sandbag annexes obviously clustered around'. As a Field Works officer, Blunden was scathing about the defences that the battalion were expected to man. Whilst the British front line was constructed in the massive canal bank 'than which a finer parapet could not be demanded', the rest of the defences were feeble [U/W p.154]. In addition, the Germans had a magnificent *minenwerfer*, 'well masked under the wreckage of a place known as Steam Mill'. Blunden's neat handwriting in the War Diary records that on 2 January 1917 the Machine Gun Tunnel completely disappeared after the attention of this much-feared weapon.

A German 25cm *Minenwerfer*, a type of which was masked under the wreckage of Steam Mill.

The Steam Mill, Boezinghe. A modern photograph taken from the bridge across the canal, on the south side of the mill. Blunden describes the bridge here as being a dangerous feature which enabled both British and German raiding parties to make unexpected sorties into each other's positions.

Another dangerous feature here was the broken railway bridge which crossed over the canal just south of Steam Mill, leading eastwards into the German lines. This 'promised two hateful excitements - the order to raid the enemy thereabouts, the receipt of a raiding party from him'. Very fierce frosts made life even more uncomfortable and more dangerous, although the 11th Royal Sussex escaped raids in either direction.

The General's solution to these conditions was to install more and more barbed wire. The noise of handling it - from the tin protection on its bobbins - meant that the wirers' position was easily betrayed, and it was an unpopular material. Blunden's much-admired NCO Sergeant Worley managed to get some wire installed, but in Blunden's view he was lucky.

On 3 January 1917 the battalion handed over to the 14th Hampshires and moved to more pleasant billets at Rossel Farm, Elverdinghe, a quiet camp west of Boesinghe. Soon after, on 10 January, the C.O. and a group of officers (including Blunden) set off by lorry to Ypres, with their first stop near the ramparts at the severely damaged Menin Gate. Here they entered the headquarters and then investigated the daunting east-facing area, studied the trenches and the sentries. They had reached Railway Wood, and the 11th Royal Sussex was to hold a section of the line here and at nearby Potizje. The battalion bombs were stored in Lancer Farm, opposite Potizje château, and the Bellewaarde stream flowed ('under the ice') past the château and fed its garden ponds. The depth of the water was measured regularly, to be aware of any tampering with the stream and potential flooding.

'January Full Moon, Ypres'
The moonlight emphasises the outlines of the ghostly jagged ruins, catching the snow on the broken buildings, while flares *'peer through the naked fire-swept windows/Mocking the fallen.'* The scene is *'uneasily quiet'* and there is *'Only the Cloth Hall sentry's challenge/to someone crunching through the frozen snows'.*

Colonel Harrison and Colonel Harvey both received awards in the New Year Honours. It was Colonel Harvey's South Wales Borderers that Blunden's battalion had recently relieved in the line, in some haste. In his neat hand-writing, Blunden made an insertion in the battalion war diary, headed ADDENDUM, giving a neatly arranged list of awards for the Royal Sussex, headed by Colonel Harrison and his new

Blunden's Friends, taken at the end of 1916. Back row *left to right*: **Lt G Maycock, MC, Transport Officer; Capt James Cassels, MC (transferred to the RFC); Lt Whitley, 'OC** *Daily Mirror'.* **Front, Capt PF Drew.**

Distinguished Service Order. Colonel Harvey of the South Wales Borderers had to be content with a mere 'mention' in the Honours List.

The 11th Sussex positions were on the north-west side of Railway Wood, towards Cambridge Road (today a minor road linking the N 8 with the N 332 roads), on 16th January. Cambridge Road itself, about 500 yards behind the British front line, ran approximately parallel with it, with two communication trenches running back from it: Haymarket and, parallel and 500 yards to the south, the important trench known as Piccadilly. Both led to another extensive communication trench, at right-angles and linking with Hellfire Corner on the Menin Road to the south. The southern boundary of the battalion sector was marked by the raised embankment of the Ypres - Zonnebeke railway line, running north-east from Ypres; later that month the battalion was to experience the dangerous cover that this provided for the enemy.

Blunden learned at about this time that he had been awarded the Military Cross. The London Gazette for 26 January 1917 records:

> *Temp. 2nd Lt. Edmund Charles Blunden. R.Sussex R. For conspicuous gallantry in action. He displayed great courage and*

Cambridge Road, showing a culvert under the road embankment (formerly the Ypres – Zonnebeke railway). On 25 January 1917 a strong German patrol used the culvert to emerge into No Man's Land within 20 yards of the British front line.

Panorama of Gully Farm, 'A sector of the northern Ypres Salient, the British trench line clearly shown in the foreground'. PT SCOTT COLLECTION

determination when in charge of a carrying party under heavy fire. He has previously done fine work.

This seems likely to relate to the action at Hamel on 3 September 1917 (see p.69 above)

There seems to be some uncertainty about the origins of the award. Two modern authorities attribute it to the events of 13 November when he lost his way and inadvertently crossed into enemy territory near the Schwaben Redoubt (see p.82-4); but on that occasion he was not involved in a carrying party whereas on 3 September his task was specifically one of carrying bombs in dangerous circumstances. Apparently when Blunden reported to the General on his return from being lost on 13 November the unexpected but welcome news was that his bravery had won him the Military Cross - but it seems more probable that his return from reconnaissance on that occasion coincided with the news that his earlier actions at Hamel with the carrying parties and previous fine work had won him an official recommendation for the Military Cross, which was gazetted two months later.

Unhelpfully, but with typical personal reticence, when writing up the war diary at the time he made no reference to his official notification of the award.

On the same date the much-admired Lieutenant-Colonel W. H. Stanway, late of the Royal Welch Fusiliers of Red Dragon Crater fame and now commanding officer of the 6th Cheshires, received a bar to his D.S.O. in recognition of his gallantry and leadership in the capture of St. Pierre Divion on 13 November 1916, the battle in which Captain R. Kirk was killed.

Army Form C. 2118.

WAR DIARY

or

INTELLIGENCE SUMMARY.

(Erase heading not required.)

Instructions regarding War Diaries and Intelligence Summaries are contained in F. S. Regs., Part II. and the Staff Manual respectively. Title pages will be prepared in manuscript.

Place	Date	Hour	Summary of Events and Information	Remarks and references to Appendices
BOESINGHE	Jan 1st		Battalion in trenches. Minenwerfers busy especially on Belgian front.	E.B.
	2nd		Minenwerfers again busy, and R.G. turned in front but invisible.	E.B.
	3rd		Am relieved without casualties by 14th HANTS and march to reserve billets at RUSSEL FARM, ELVERDINGHE.	E.B.
RUSSEL FM	4th		Am relieved. Brigade goes to Corps HQ. Capt. R.H. Lupton goes to Corps HQ.	E.B.
	5th		Rest and cleaning. Brigade working-parties supplied. In evening Camp maintenance and improvements begun.	E.B.
	6th		Working parties continued. Capt. E.H. Mant D.S.O. takes over duties as M.O. vice Capt. Milne (to M.A.C.)	E.B.
	7th		Working parties.	E.B.
			Divine Service under Capt. Thorn. M.C. Subsections	E.B.
	8th		Working parties.	E.B.
	9th		2nd Lieut. J. Corbett takes over duties as Adjutant. Rann employed in Railway Construction all day.	E.B.
	10th		Railway Construction. Reconnoitring party sent to the RAILWAY WOOD SECTOR of the YPRES salient.	E.B.
	11th		The same.	E.B.
	12th		The same.	E.B.
	13th			E.B.
	14th		Heather Ahmed. Railway construction impossible. Inspection in billets.	E.B.
YPRES	15th		Sunday. No working parties required.	E.B.
POTIJZE	16th		Battalion marches after dark into YPRES and rests in the cellars of the CONVENT and houses near the STATION	E.B.
			Battalion marches up by night to relieve 2/8th KING'S LIVERPOOL (IRISH) in RAILWAY WOOD LEFT. H.Q. in POTIJZE CHAT grounds.	E.B.
			Relief successfully carried out and reported complete 9.20 p.m.	E.B.
YPRES	17th		Heavy snow. Last day. Guns. Fatigue. Ross join Pt. Van Eston BAYNARD (transferred to C.C.S.) Officers' patrols sent out.	E.B.
	18th		New Snowy. Backs again quiet. Mr again shows up well in support patrols.	E.B.
	19th		Quiet. I saw wounded by sniper. Heavy do good work late am. V-system. Quieing. Patrols continued.	E.B.
	20th		Day Quiet. In this evening Am relieved by 14th HANTS and return with relish in CONVENT & near STATION YPRES	E.B.
	21st		2nd Lt. Cassy join the Pa. Working. Parties supplied for work on CAMBRIDGE TRENCH and wiring in front of X LINE	E.B.

Comdg. 11th Royal Sussex Regt.

for. Lt. Col.

Comdg. 11th Royal Sussex Regt.

War Diary, 11th Royal Sussex – a typical set of entries written up by Edmund Blunden – in January 1917.

With occasional reliefs from other battalions in the Division, the 11th Royal Sussex continued to hold this stretch of the front line. By the end of January the war diary no longer bore Blunden's neat handwriting with his initials at the end of each day's entry; his friend Arnold Vidler took over as writer, and Blunden was now Intelligence Officer.

Life was not comfortable. It was bitterly cold, as winter 'came out fierce and determined; first there was a heavy snow, then the steel-blue sky of hard frost'. Blunden had an opportunity to reconnoitre in Ypres itself and the trenches they were to hold:

> *The sad Salient lay under a heavy silence, broken here and there by the ponderous muffled thump of trench mortar shells round the line.... There was in the town itself the same strange silence, and the staring pallor of the streets in that daybreak was unlike anything that I had known. The Middle Ages had here contrived to lurk, and this was their torture at last.* [U/W, p.156]

The front line was crude and the front-line parapet gave very little protection, so low that men had stoop as they walked along the trenches. The front line had no dug-outs, and very few recesses for storing ammunition. Ahead was a flimsy wire defence, with a similarly unimpressive line of German wire beyond. As was usually the case, the Germans occupied the higher ground but nevertheless in the distance beyond their line certain 'bony remains' could be identified, such as Oskar Farm and Wilde Wood. This was the Potijze sector.

Several patrols went out into No Man's Land in the first few days of February 1917. Reports from 'an absolutely reliable Belgium source' indicated that preparations were in hand for a German offensive, and alertness was essential. Blunden felt that the frequent patrolling was foolhardy and mentions his 'Old Blues' Vidler and Amon, skilled in this type of activity, lying out in the bitter cold and listening to German sentries talking. The crucial need for alertness was emphasised by Colonel Harrison; Blunden was startled on one occasion to see the colonel's 'merciless arrest' of a sentry who defied orders and protected his freezing ears with a knitted comforter. Anything that interfered with his hearing could be disastrous if he failed to hear an approaching enemy raid, and he was endangering the lives of everyone in the trench, including himself. No Man's Land in this bitter cold winter demanded 'desperate energy' from the wiring parties as they strained

> *to screw their pickets into the granite. The men lying at each listening-post were freezing stiff, and would take half an hour's buffeting and rubbing on return to avoid becoming casualties.*

Moonlight, steely and steady, flooded the flat space between us and the Germans. [U/W, p.160]

The need for vigilance was demonstrated towards the end of January when a German patrol raided one of the battalion's bombing posts in some strength, and with great ingenuity. Casualties were three men missing, five dead from wounds and several others who suffered slight wounds, although the raiders had suffered deaths too, one still clutching the wooden handle of a stick bomb. It was a cleverly-designed raid, for the railway embankment running close to Railway Wood and marking the southern limit of the battalion's front, had provided cover for the enemy until their bombardment began, when the raiders emerged from an unobserved culvert for their attack.

Blunden decided to look at the devastation caused by the enemy bombardment and the raid, and crossed an isolated trench near Gully Farm, close to the Ypres - Zonnebeke railway line with Railway Wood beyond it. He found the bombing post crushed and demolished, its existence blurred into the surrounding wilderness, with an unexploded shell lying beside it [U/W, p.164]. At Potijze Château the frozen bodies of the German raiders were stripped of their underwear; HQ wanted to see specimens of underclothing of standard German issue for purposes of comparison.

Two of Blunden's men (Privates Page and Babbage) undertook this disagreeable task, and had to 'hew it off the frozen bodies'. Blunden too, as battalion intelligence officer, had to venture into No Man's Land. The ground to be crossed by some of the patrols was covered with snow and an order came through that patrols should wear white suits. As Blunden commented privately, 'None being available, a number of pretty night-dresses were sent up by some genius'. (The 'genius' was Lieutenant and Quartermaster Swain.)

It was part of the Battalion Intelligence Officer's duties to know all about the houses that lay within the British lines, along the Potijze - Zonnebeke road. Blunden 'conceived a liking for many of them, a smithy here, a summer-house or a lodge there and one red-brick dwelling with a bassinette, a supply of tracts on Sunday observance, two sewing-machines .... there was an insistent echo of old life still, and the gate-pillars signalised the definite ownership of certain large, ornamented but heavily mortgaged buildings' [U/W p.166]. Echoes of English village life can be heard across the devastation of Flanders.

Looking to the north from the château across the Bellewaarde stream, Blunden could see the church of Saint

Jean (Sint Jan) about half a mile away, beside the crossroads on the Ypres - Wieltje road. The tower was damaged but still stood, 'in shining prominence'. To the south, again about half a mile away, he could see Hellfire Corner and 'a suburb of tallish red houses' along the dangerous Menin Road.

February 1917 was a time of reorganisation and specialist training. The 11th Royal Sussex left Potijze and moved to Brandhoek on the Ypres - Poperinghe road for training, two companies were detailed to support the 16th Battalion Rifle Brigade in a raid on Railway Wood, Colonel Harrison returned from an Army School course, and on the 16th the battalion arrived at Bollezeele, north-east of St. Omer, described as 'untouched and sociable'. Here Blunden was working with Sergeant Worley on a new plan for setting up barbed wire quickly; the Divisional General visited, inspected, and approved, enquired about Blunden's age and service, and remarked to the colonel on the subaltern with impressive boots (a pair of large new Wellingtons) and rapid efficiency with the barbed wire. After this interlude the battalion moved back to Ypres, though not before enjoying an 'officers' reunion' in the officers' mess one evening and an evening concert in the sergeants' mess.

'Concert Party, Busseboom' [U/W, p.252]
Perhaps it was this concert that inspired a deceptive poem that lulls the reader into comfortable contemplation of men at rest, enjoying music and laughter with dance, jest and rhythm. Yet Blunden gives notice immediately that we are not entirely off duty, and each stanza has its warning; already in the second line of the poem there is an ambiguous note: *'The stage was set, the house was packed/The famous troop began;'* - using the word 'troop' for the concert party performers, or troupe, holds attention on the surrounding reality despite the cheering

Ruins in Ypres – two views from Blunden's album showing the Cloth Hall and St Martin's church.

music-hall atmosphere. The purely enjoyable part of the show is soon dealt with and reality creeps in again with 'the maniac blast' of 'another matinée', the audible and visible barrage not far away 'called madness'. The poem ends with a chilling ferocity like many of Siegfried Sassoon's poems:

> To this new concert, white we stood;
> Cold certainty held our breath;
> While men in the tunnels below Larch Wood
> Were kicking men to death.

Their new posting was the Observatory Ridge Sector, on rising ground in Sanctuary Wood with Zillebeke behind them and Valley Cottages close by. It was not an encouraging location, and as usual the Germans were occupying the higher ground. On 28 February the British front line trenches came under heavy fire in the evening, from minenwerfer, rifle fire and artillery. SOS signals brought down retaliatory fire from the British artillery, and after an hour all was quiet again, but the 11th Royal Sussex had suffered two soldiers killed, and two officers and 11 O.R.s wounded. At Valley Cottages the battalion headquarters had suffered heavy shelling, and R.S.M. Daniels was mortally wounded and died a few days later in the Casualty Clearing Station in Vlamertinghe.

By this time Lieutenant-Colonel Harrison had handed over command of the battalion to Major Millward and returned to England. Before leaving, he arranged for Blunden to be made Brigade Intelligence Officer - so the young man who less than nine months ago had joined the battalion in the line at Festubert as an inexperienced second lieutenant was now, a full lieutenant and holder of a Military Cross, to be on the brigade staff.

'Concert Party, Busseboom'. The photograph, taken at the actual location of the concert party at Schaapstal (between Busseboom and Reningelst), shows the view eastwards. The barrage from St Eloi would be clearly visible, lighting up the sky. Two church spires help to orientate the viewer, their tips just visible above the horizon – Vlamertinghe on the left, Dikkebus on the right.

VLAMERTINGHE

DIKKEBUS

The Lille Gate, Ypres, autumn 1917 and 1999: Well within range of the German artillery, casualties were suffered here from time to time. It was near the Lille Gate that Blunden as Brigade Intelligence Officer occupied an old brick vault in the Ramparts.

Despite the advancement, Blunden was not entirely happy at leaving his friends. Second Lieutenants Lintott and Vidler had both been evacuated to hospital, his friend Cassels had transferred to the Royal Flying Corps, and he felt 'in a void' Nevertheless he settled down to discover what was required of him: he had to compile all the information gleaned from various sources at the front and then write daily reports to be sent to HQ 39th Division and circulated amongst the other units in 116 Brigade. Perhaps the clarity and conciseness of the battalion war diary entries that Blunden wrote had impressed Brigade and resulted in his appointment. He was directly responsible for observation posts and snipers' lairs and 'could now claim to be a bureaucrat, for there were two clerks to draw maps and produce manifold copies of reports and programmes' [U/W p.171].

Notwithstanding this clerkly atmosphere, Brigade was by no means a safe location. The headquarters 'was compendiously concealed' in a vault under the ramparts of Ypres, near the Lille Gate - but not far enough, as Blunden observed, for although they were behind the lines men were occasionally killed by shell-fire. The frequent visits to sections of the front line were a daily danger.

A typical trench visit involved leaving Ypres by the Lille Gate and crossing the moat onto the exposed flat land beyond, towards Zillebeke Lake, risking artillery fire used to snipe even single individuals. A precarious battery position lay along the Ypres - Zonnebeke railway here, then numerous shanties and holes dug into the banks of the Zillebeke Lake dam, and the lake itself contained sunken boats. The corner of the lake was camouflaged, and a communication trench led into the village of Zillebeke itself, eventually reaching the church via Hallebast Corner - naturally soon known as Hellblast Corner by the troops. Even then it had a number of wooden crosses, now long since replaced by more permanent CWGC headstones that commemorate those of the Grenadier Guards and Household Cavalry who died here in November 1914, in attacks from Observatory Ridge and Sanctuary Wood.

A battalion headquarters was established in Valley Cottages, and visitors were briefly in full sight of German observers as they moved from Zillebeke Street to the back door of the HQ. Although many areas in Flanders could not provide secure deep dugouts, because of the very high water-table, the front line supports here began with very deep dugouts.

Hellblast Corner, Zillebeke, 1917 and 1999. Blunden made several journeys along a communication trench through this area. Zillebeke lake is on the right; note the 'shanties' built into the bank. (IWM, E.Aus 4611)

The country child at Blunden's heart still saw the rural setting that the war was destroying. In 'Zillebeke Brook', written in the spring of 1917, he observed how

This muddy water chuckling in its run
Takes wefts of colour from the April sun,
And paints for fancy's eye a glassy burn
Ribanded through a brake of Kentish fern ...

The church at Brielen. Blunden's battalion often marched past this church as they left the trenches on their way to camp at Elverdinghe. Blunden bought this postcard in 1917 when, as he says, 'you could still see the date on the church before the Passchendaele upheaval.'

BRIELEN — De kerk - L'église - Church voor't bombardement

1 3 9

Uitgever Sansen-Vannesle, Poperinghe Verb-Nadruk

Bought 1917, when you could still see the date on the church, before the Paschendaele upheaval

The Trois Tours Chateau, Brielen, pictured after the war when it was the headquarters of the Ypres League and the Anglo-Belgian Union.

Another battalion Headquarters was at a little hillock called Rudkin House, facing Hill 60, installed in the mouth of an old well with a tunnelled dugout at its bottom. The cookhouse and its wood-smoke further reduced the air supply in a tunnel that was already not well ventilated. Rudkin House, however, had a safe communication trench leading to the front line. On one occasion Blunden was accompanying the Brigade Major, Major Clark, when they were both astonished to see British troops fleeing from the emergency exits between the front and support line systems, surrounded by rising smoke: even the enemy gunners were so taken aback by the sight that they failed to take advantage of the situation - a machine-gunner had failed to distinguish between a can of water and a can of petrol. Tunnel fires of this kind were not unusual, and cost a number of lives; on this particular occasion one man died of suffocation [U/W, p.176].

April brought the battalion ten days' rest at Poperinghe, but they were back in the line again by 18 April, this time in dugouts along the Yser canal north of Ypres. Here they were close to a pretty house called Reigersburg Château, west of the canal and south of Brielen, on the Ypres - Elverdinghe road, and another, the Château des Trois Tours. Both these houses were unexpectedly free from enemy fire, but the village of Brielen itself was no more than a series of brick mounds.

Visit: Ypres and the surrounding area provide plenty of reminders of Blunden's war experience. Around the time of his centenary (1996), plaques were set up in several sites, displaying his poems with local reference:
- beside the inner courtyard door of the Cloth Hall, in Ypres itself (next to the entrance to the 'In Flanders Fields' museum);
- outside Vlamertinghe château, between Ypres and Poperinghe;

THE BRIDGE HILL 60 IN 1916·—FROM GERMAN FRONT LINE.

[The British front line seen through the arch. Hill 60 itself is on the right.

Two pictures of Hill 60: from Edmund Blunden's album, in 1916, seen through the arch of a bridge from the German front line, and as it appeared after 1918.

- outside the museum at Hooge;
- and on the Ypres ramparts, close to the Menin Gate.

Leave Ypres on road N 369, for Boesinghe (Boezinge), go under road N 38, and stop at Essex Farm Cemetery, on the right of the road. Among its many graves are those of a fifteen-year-old boy, Private Strudwick, and a Victoria Cross winner, Private Barrett. Take the path to see the concrete shelters in the embankment of the Yser Canal. On several occasions Blunden's battalion crossed the canal by Bridge No. 4, close at hand, on their way to and from the front lines.

Continue along the N 369. Just before Boezinge, turn right across the canal bridge, signposted Langemark and Poelkapelle. The Steam Mill is on the left as you cross the bridge. Follow the road round to the right towards Pilkem (ignoring the small road next to

Three pictures of permanent displays of Edmund Blunden poems: beside the entrance door to the 'In Flanders Fields' museum, the Cloth Hall, Ypres ('Les Halles d'Ypres'); on the wall of the Hooge military museum ('Trench Raid near Hooge'); and outside the château gates in Vlamertinghe, ('Vlamertinghe, passing the château'). The 'In Flanders Fields' museum in the Cloth Hall makes extensive use of Blunden's poems and comments about the war.

Trench Raid near Hooge

At an hour before the rosy-fingered
Morning should come
To wonder again what meant these sties.
These wailing shots, these glaring eyes,
These moping mum.

Through the black reached strange long rosy fingers
All at one aim
Protending, and bending down they swept,
Successions of similars after leapt
And bore red flame

To one small ground of the eastern distance,
And thunderous touched,
East then and west false dawns fan-flashed
And shut, and gaped, false thunders clashed,
Who stood and watched

Caught piercing horror from the desperate pit
Which with ten men
Was centre of this. The blood burnt, feeling
The fierce truth there and the last appealing,
"Us? Us? Again?"

Nor rosy dawn at last appearing
Through the icy shade
Might mark without trembling the new deforming
Of earth that had seemed past further storming,
Her fingers played.

One thought, with something of human pity
On six or seven
Whose looks were hard to understand,
But that they ceased to care what hand
Lit earth and heaven.

EDMUND BLUNDEN (1896 – 1974)

Vlamertinghe
Passing the Chateau. July 1917

"And all her silken flanks with garlands drest"—
But we are coming to the sacrifice.
Must those have flowers who are not yet gone West?
May those have flowers who live with death and lice?
This must be the floweriest place
That earth allows; the queenly face
Of the proud mansion borrows grace for grace
Spite of those brute guns lowing at the skies.

Bold great daisies, golden lights,
Bubbling roses' pinks and, whites—
Such a gay carpet! poppies by the million,
Such damask! such vermilion!
But if you ask me, mate, the choice of colour
Is scarcely right; this red should have been duller.

EDMUND BLUNDEN, (1896 – 1974)

Les Halles d'Ypres

A TANGLE of iron rods and spluttered beams.
On brickwork past the skill of a mason to mend.
A wall with a bright blue poster – odd as dreams
Is the city's latter end.

A shapeless obelisk looms Saint Martin's spire,
Now a lean aiming-mark for the German guns;
And the Cloth Hall crouches beside, disfigured with fire.
The glory of Flanders once.

Only the foursquare tower still bears the trace
Of beauty that was, and strong embattled age.
And gilded ceremonies and pride of place –
Before this senseless rage.

And still you may see (below the noon serene,
The mysterious, changeless vault of sharp blue light),
The pigeons come to the tower, and flaunt and preen,
And flicker in playful flight.

EDMUND BLUNDEN (1896 – 1974)

the canal and a minor road going straight ahead after the Mill). After about a mile turn right at the crossroads (signposted Ieper), into Pilkemseweg, and continue to Vijfwegen just under a mile away. Turn left here at the small crossroads, into Vanheulestraat and then immediately right into Moortelweg; go past a path after about half a mile, leading to No Man's Cot cemetery, then follow the road as it bears to the left and then to the right. Go straight over the next crossroads, into what was known as Admiral's Road.

Beside the crossroads, stop and look towards the farm straight ahead: the shallow valley immediately to the right is the area where

Brigade Headquarters at No. 4 Bridge, Essex Farm. This well-known place became a familiar sight on the occasions when the battalion held the Canal Bank sector in 1916 and 1917. Lieutenant-Colonel J M McCrae, Royal Canadian Medical Corps, famous for his poem 'In Flanders Fields', was here in 1915.

Blunden's battalion formed up for the attack on St. Julien on 31 July 1917. A little way off to the left was the German front line, in particular Calf Avenue, Caliban Support and Calf Reserve, where Blunden and his signallers dug themselves in. Continue straight ahead, cross over the very busy N 38 and then the N 313, into the village of Wieltje. At the T-junction turn right (there is a CWGC sign to Oxford Road Cemetery), then almost immediately left into Wieltjesstraat, Oxford Road.

Carry straight on, and at the junction with the N 332 turn right into Zonnesbeeksweg; there is a French military cemetery on the left. Almost immediately, turn sharp left down the road that runs alonside the French cemetery (Begijnenbosstraat): this was known to the British Army as Cambridge Road.

You are now in the British lines of 1917, with No Man's Land on your left. It was from here that Blunden made his way to the wrecked trenches of Gully Farm after the German raid of 25 January 1917. Gully Farm was in the British lines; its modern successor lies in the clump of trees to your right as you look at No Man's Land. The wood beyond and to the right of the farm is Railway Wood.

Continue along Cambridge Road (Begijnenbosstraaat), cross over the busy main Ypres - Zonnebeke road, which was a railway embankment until a few years ago, and continue straight ahead alongside Railway Wood. With the wood on your left, take a left turn at the far end and follow it along Oudekortrijkstraat (CWGC sign, R.E. Grave Railway Wood); park on the right to walk up the slight rise to the memorial.

At this point it is worth walking on a little further, to the end of Railway Wood, for the view over not only Gully Farm and Cambridge Road but also the culverts running under the modern main road - the former railway track: it is possible that one of these was used in the German raid on the Royal Sussex trenches on 25 January 1917.

Return to the car, continue past Railway Wood and after about quarter of a mile turn sharp left into Oude Bellewarde straat. Cross over the Ypres - Zonnebeke road and at the next main road, N 332 (Zonne Beeke Weg), turn left to Potijze, the location of the 11th Royal Sussex Headquarters.

Turn left at the roundabout in Potijze, into Kruiskal Sijdestraat, signposted Zillebeke, and continue to the roundabout at Hellfire Corner on the Menin Road.

Depending on the time available, turn right down the Menin Road to return to Ypres or left towards Hooge to continue the battlefield visit (continued on page 134).

Whilst the 11th Royal Sussex was installed along the canal, Blunden's duties took him to his old battalion. Here he met Arnold Vidler once more, who brought him news of yet another 'Old Blue' in the battalion,

Ernest Tice. This brought the Christ's Hospital eventual representation in the battalion to five - Blunden, Vidler, Collyer, Amon, and now Tice.

Blunden was now rich enough in experience to feel confident of his judgement of senior officers, and still youthfully reckless enough to express his opinions in the presence of a 'highly conservative general'. Some outspoken and inappropriate remarks, concerning both military and non-military matters, were less than well received by his superiors (although the General read Blunden's poems 'with great pleasure'). His Brigade Major, Major Clark, supported the proposal that this quick-minded and articulate young man should leave his Intelligence post and return to regimental duty, as he fervently wished to do; by 1 May 1917 Lieutenant Blunden, MC, was back with the 11th Royal Sussex, out of the line in St. Omer, 'a genuine infantryman and with less enthusiasm than was apparent' [U/W, p.187].

The area round St. Omer was ideal for training large numbers of troops, and the town itself was charming; even in wartime its beautifully laid-out parks were kept in irreproachable condition, and the atmosphere was cheerful and cosmopolitan.

Activities here for the 11th Royal Sussex in May 1917 began with exercises at platoon level, and Blunden plodded through the surrounding countryside to 'outflank a prearranged and harmless enemy'. Lodged in billets in various villages round the town, the troops took part in mock attacks and route marches, in platoon, company, battalion and finally Brigade strength.

While Blunden was absent, first on rest and then on a musketry course, the battalion moved to Wormhoudt, north-east of St. Omer and west of Poperinghe, for final inspections before returning to the front line on 28 May 1917. These inspections were impressive: first, the 'cooks and cookers', followed by further inspections by Warrant Officers and NCOs in descending order of seniority - Regimental Sergeant Major, Company Sergeant-Majors and Company Quartermaster Sergeants, and finally the battalion chiropodists. As a grand conclusion the battalion was inspected overall by the Brigade Commander, Brigadier-General Hornby - and they were passed ready for front line service.

Blunden caught up with his battalion at Brigade Reserve on the Canal Bank East sector, and in making his way to the headquarters just avoided a shell which had landed in a communication trench nearby, killing two runners and narrowly missing his friend Sergeant Davey. Ypres was shelled heavily during the night of 6-7 June, and the battalion reported: 'Big operation on our right at 3.10 am'. This was the start of the Battle of Messines which had begun with nineteen British mines exploding beneath the German lines. Many lives were lost, in a scene described by a German observer as like 'nineteen gigantic roses with carmine petals', while a British eye-witness saw 'great leaping streams of orange flame'.

Full military discipline continued in all circumstances, front line duty and mine explosions notwithstanding, for the next day saw a Field General Court Martial of a young 11th Royal Sussex officer - Second Lieutenant W. R. Botting, who had been with the battalion for a mere six weeks. No indication of the charge appears in the War Diary, but four days later it records his return to 'B' Company, having been 'severely censured'.

Towards the end of June the 11th Royal Sussex was back in the St. Omer area once more, this time at Houille for intensive training to prepare for the forthcoming Flanders offensive. There was a happy day for the battalion's Old Blues - Vidler, Amon, Collyer, Tice and Blunden - to explore the old town, roaming through the streets and the cathedral 'with such exhilarations of wit and irony that we felt no other feast like this could ever come again'. Their forebodings were justified, for Collyer and Tice were both to die within the next six weeks, in the attack at St. Julien.

The battalion returned to Poperinghe and the noise of war: a working party discovered that the ammunition depot had been destroyed by enemy fire, and on 20 June a large ammunition dump in Vlamertinghe was hit by enemy shelling and set alight, so that the shells crackled all night long.

In his oblique way, Blunden indicates that he was suffering from strain. After dreadful days and nights around Vlamertinghe, he was caught on his way back from inspecting the front line by a barrage in which 'shells struck so fast that we seemed to be one shell-hole away, and no more, from the latest'; after this

we were not much good for observation or offence, and found out no more. On our shaky way down from the line ...we quickly found that we should have chosen any other route ... we beheld in the sickening brightness a column of artillery waggons, noiseless, smashed, capsized, the remains of mules and drivers sprawling among the wreckage ... I called upon the Canal Bank Major, who was normally in control of the accommodations. No sooner was I inside the sandbag porch of his lair than a shell knocked the porch in, and some more of my nerve system with it. [U/W, p. 195-6]

The Yser Canal at Essex Farm Cemetery. The canal banks were full of tunnels and dug-outs used by the British as shelters. After the battalion came out of the attack at St Julien in July 1917, the second in command of the 11th Royal Sussex put the survivors of the attack under cover in dug-outs along the canal bank; it is believed that the canal banks still contain tunnels, their entrances long since blocked in.

> Physically, although Blunden was never wounded, he suffered from attacks of asthma, a life-long complaint exacerbated by occasional encounters with gas shells (and also by smoking). Like everyone else engaged in the war, he suffered the constant pain of the loss of friends - losses and experiences which returned to him throughout his life. It was a heavy burden at the age of 20.

31 July 1917 was one of the dates that remained vivid in Blunden's memory all his life. The battalion moved up the line in the Hill Top sector on 28 July, to a position just north-west of Wieltje. The sector was on a slight ridge running east-west at right angles to the front line and stretching for just under a mile to the north of St. Jean with its eastern end in the British-held village of Wieltje. The Germans were clearly expecting an attack; active fire inflicted sixteen casualties on the battalion in the British communication trenches during the next two days. At La Brique, about a mile north of Ypres, Blunden saw a number of bodies - casualties from other battalions on their way to the front. As they approached the front line on 30 July, Tice went one way and Blunden another. Tice died of wounds two days later.

The 11th Royal Sussex was about to join in the Flanders offensive, an operation which had started on 7 June 1917 with the Battle of Messines, and was to continue with various breaks until 10 November 1917. Blunden's battalion was in the 116th Brigade, serving with the 12th and 13th Royal Sussex and the 14th Hampshires. Together with two other brigades they formed the 39th Division. The object of the offensive was to free north-west Belgium from enemy occupation. The attack of 31 July had been delayed, partly owing to the tremendous preparations necessary, mostly in areas overlooked by the Germans,

After the War.
The canal lost itself in the later stages, but when we first saw it was broad, & real water.

Some of the bridge-building on the canal in the summer of 1917.

Two views of the canal, in the summer of 1917 and after the war. Two views from Edmund Blunden's album.

and partly to give the French time for their operation in freeing part of Belgium. It was also intended to distract German attention from the French whose armies had mutined further south (in the Chemin des Dames offensive). Three armies were concerned in the Flanders offensive - the Second and Fifth British armies and the First French army.

By the time the Third Battle of Ypres petered out in the mud and shell-cratered ground of Passchendaele in November 1917, when there was no realistic prospect of any further advance, it had involved the British and Dominions in over a quarter of a million casualties. Some of these were the result of enemy bombing and shelling of medical establishments and casualty clearing stations behind the lines.

The unfolding events involved the 11th Royal Sussex, including Edmund Blunden, throughout the remainder of 1917, and brought the battalion into some dreadful actions. First came the Battle of Pilckem, which was to occupy two days and cost the battalion 275 casualties (including the lives of Blunden's 'Old Blue' friends Collyer and Tice). On 30 July 1917 Blunden's 116 Brigade, under Brigadier-General Hornby, had taken up their battle position on the British front line (facing north-east) just west of Admiral's Road and north-west from Wieltje towards Boesinghe. The 117th Brigade was on their left, the 118th Brigade stood in reserve to the rear; two brigades of the 51st Highland Division were on the left of the 117th Brigade, and three brigades of the 55th Division immediately on the right of the 116th. The furthest left of these three lay west of the continuing Admiral's Road up to its junction in the village of Wieltje.

The first objective of the 116th and 117th Brigades beyond No Man's Land was to take and occupy the lightly-held German front-line systems, then to form a line stretching from the corner of Kitchener's Wood to a point just south of St. Julien on the Wieltje - Poelcappelle road, known as Corner Cot.

This was a formidable assignment, for the main trenches to be attacked were strongly held, well fortified with concrete 'pill box' shelters equipped with machine guns. Units of the 118th Brigade were to pass through, to take up positions on the eastern bank of the River Steenbeek where the German main force was ready to counter-attack if the British advance hesitated.

The 39th Division did well, although the cost was severe - the 4th/5th Black Watch, for example, suffered 336 casualties. Unfortunately the 2/5th Lancashire Fusiliers, in the 55th Division, were held up in their advance, leaving their neighbours dangerously exposed; and not only did the Royal Sussex and others therefore come under heavy enemy machine-gun fire from their flanks but, at a later stage, some of the 39th Division were actually shot from behind by Germans still holding positions to their rear.

The 13th Royal Sussex were particularly successful, the battalion

1914-15... SAINT-JULIEN (Langemarck)
Beschoten Kerk - Église bombardée - Bombarded Church

The 39ᵗʰ Divⁿ took the site, 31 July 1917

1914-15 — SAINT-JULIEN (Langemark)
Het Dorp - Le Village - The Village

But not 1917. Then, nil.

Two views of St Julien, church and village. His friends Collyer and Tice lost their lives here.

115

capturing 17 German officers and 205 Other Ranks; but they also suffered casualties, some at Van Heule Farm. (Blunden describes these events in *Undertones of War,* pages 198-206, in terms which leave no doubt of the alarms, noise, cold, fears and wretched conditions of the battle.) In the end, however, it was impossible to hold on to St. Julien and some of the area beyond; the survivors had to fall back just south of the village, forming up on the eastern bank of the River Steenbeek where the banks - five feet high - formed a useful form of defence.

The opening day of the battle, 31 July, began extremely early, with the men of the 11th Royal Sussex enjoying a substantial breakfast of sausages, bacon, coffee and rum at 1.30 a.m. Just before 4 a.m. the battle began: 'a flooded Amazon of steel flowed roaring' over their heads [U/W, p.198].

Blunden was in charge of the battalion signallers. Designated as specialists, these men were usually considered to have an enviable appointment with the minimum of fatigues and the maximum of time in battalion HQ. However true this may have been of static trench warfare, in battle the task of maintaining telephone contact between units was onerous and frequently dangerous. Reels of telephone wire had to be run out from battalion HQ, the linesmen paying out the wire as

REs taking up wire. IWM Q6050

they followed the advancing infantry across No Man's Land. Inevitably the wire was cut by shell-fire from time to time, often in several places at once, and a signaller had to trace the wire until the break was found and then repair it, frequently under fire.

As they set out from their battalion headquarters, Blunden's party scrambled across No Man's Land - finding it comparatively straightforward, and the once-fearful German wire 'puny' - and 'blundered' across the facing trench [U/W, p.198]. Two of Blunden's signallers were wounded, and he 'was left to bandage them in my own ineffective way'.

The signallers soon came in touch with the battalion companies digging in on the captured German trenches: Caliban Support, Calf Avenue, Calf Reserve - no longer German trenches, they were now no more than rural barriers of brushwood and hurdles. Unlike 1916 conditions, there were few enemy dead to be seen, for by this time it was German practice to keep the front lines lightly manned, with the main strength farther back.

The capture of these trenches was not without loss, however, for two more of Blunden's men were killed outright, and later he learned of the death of his friend Collyer while crossing No Man's Land - and on the second day of the battle another of the 'Old Blue' set of friends, Second Lieutenant Tice, was severely wounded in a struggle with two Germans who were evacuating a dugout. He died later of his wounds and is buried in Brandhoek New Military Cemetery, Vlamertinghe.

Remembering two 'Old Blues': Tice's grave at Brandhoek Cemetery and Collyer's name on the Menin Gate.

WRIGLEY W.

ROYAL SUSSEX REGIMENT

LIEUT COLONEL	SECOND LIEUT.
RISPIN H. T.	COLLYER W. J.
	COMPTON G.
CAPTAIN	CROFT L. R.
WILSON C. A. G.	FISHER W. F.
	MARILLIER F. C. J.
LIEUTENANT	MOORE G.
DUKE B. P.	SHAW C. F.
FERGUSON J. A. R.	
LOUSADA E. A.	SERJEANT
WESTALL R. C.	BOURNE C. W.
	DELANEY M.
SECOND LIEUT	JAMES F.
BAZELEY R. A.	KERSWILL A. H.

SECOND LIEUTENANT
E W TICE
ROYAL SUSSEX REGIMENT
1ST AUGUST 1917 AGE 26

'Vlamertinghe: Passing the Château, July, 1917'
The sonnet opens with an echo from Keats's 'Ode on a
Grecian Urn', with a note of sober warning behind it:
'And all her silken flanks with garlands drest' -
But we are coming to the sacrifice.
Blunden looks at the flowers round the château, for those *'who
are not yet gone West'* and those *'who live with death and lice'*:
'bold great daisies', 'bubbling roses' - and *'poppies by the
million'*: yet he questions the bright colours, *'such vermilion!'*
*- But if you ask me, mate, the choice of colour
Is scarcely right; this red should have been duller.*
The darker shade of spilled blood would be more appropriate,
even in the flourishing garden.

Vlamertinghe Church. On the Ypres—Poperinghe Road, April, 1916.
Not much changed, Dec. 1916

Tanks wound their way through the battalion's position, on their way to support the 13th Royal Sussex in their efforts to capture St. Julien [U/W, p.199], while the battalion headquarters were squashed into a small concrete dugout in the German lines. Brigade headquarters staff arrived soon after, but then withdrew because of the intensity of enemy fire.

A severe storm of rain swept across the field, and tempers were touchy - Blunden at one point even threatened a warrant officer with arrest for the opinions he

Vlamertinghe Château, the poem displayed at the gate and the church.

was expressing. The 11th Royal Sussex withdrew from St. Julien and moved to the new front line along the banks of the Steenbeck, where they relieved the 14th Hampshires. They arrived at the new battalion headquarters just as a shell had

> blown in some concrete shelters, and killed and wounded several of our predecessors; I was aware of mummy-like half-bodies, and struggling figures, crying and cursing. [U/W, p.202]

Blunden was now in a concrete shelter along one of the trenches, and describes in *Undertones of War* [page 203] how a tank officer looked in to seek help in salvaging some equipment from his derelict tank just behind the shelter. As the battalion doctor, Captain J. H. C. Gatchell RAMC, joined them in the shelter, it received a direct hit from a 5.9 shell, landing on the concrete outside the shelter, just above Blunden's head. The doctor collapsed to the floor, the adjutant as well, and Colonel Millward staggered out, scarcely knowing where he was. Miraculously, all escaped (see below, left).

Enemy shelling increased during the afternoon of 2 August: the Regimental Aid Post, the signallers' dugout and battalion HQ were all

Edmund Blunden's pill box sketch. During the battle for St Julien the battalion commander, Lieutenant-Colonel Millward, the doctor, Captain Gatchell, the Adjutant 'Ginger' Lewis, Blunden and a tank officer were in a pill-box when it received a direct hit from a German 5.9 shell. This is how Blunden depicted the incident.

Blunden's sketch and description of HQ pill-box where a shell burst in the doorway. (see page 120)

The H.Q. was, as H.J. White tells me, a pillbox with an inner apartment.

The shell entered the narrow doorway at the moment when the staff of another battalion's H.Q. were relieving the 13th. The officers were in the little sideroom. One was blinded with a splinter. There was not much noise. The men in the large apartment were almost all killed, more by concussion than wounds.

Van Heule Farm, (St Julien) – Here the Battalion H.Q. 13th Royal Sussex, suffered 30 casualties from a shell, including Major Bartlett.

destroyed, and Blunden was the only headquarters officer still in a fit state to operate. He was able to call up the artillery by field telephone just before the line was broken: the artillery responded and the enemy fire soon slackened off [U/W, p.204].

It was about this time that another tragic incident affected Blunden deeply. A sister battalion, the 13th Royal Sussex, had established its battalion HQ in a gun-pit at Van Heule Farm on the St. Julien - Wieltje road, on the right flank of the 11th Royal Sussex just south of Corner Cot, one of the objectives of the first day of the attack. Major Cyril Bartlett rang through to Blunden's position to say that their headquarters had been pierced by a great shell, and over thirty men were dead or wounded. There seemed very little to be done, but an RAMC ambulance driver managed to reach the farm along the shell-torn St. Julien road. Major Bartlett died of his wounds three months later.

The 11th Royal Sussex were relieved on 3 August, and moved off to the comparative safety of the Yser canal, north of Ypres. They were met by the battalion Second in Command, Major Frank Cassells, retained on the canal bank so that he could take over if Colonel Millward, the C.O., should become a casualty. In this rough and ready form of home they were thankful to be under cover, in safety, and to be welcomed with a hot meal.

Better than this, however, was that the whole of the 39th Division was to leave the battle for a rest; Blunden set off to arrange accommodation, personally heartened by the further news that he was to go on leave.

Notes and Sources
'January Full Moon, Ypres', Poems 1914-30, Cobden Sanderson, 1930

Chapter Six

YPRES, 1917

**'The time too crowded for the heart to count
All the sharp cost in friends killed on the assault.'
from 'Third Ypres',** *Undertones of War*

While Blunden was on leave in August 1917, the Division was transferred from XVIII Corps in the Fifth Army to the Second Army and X Corps. This change of attachment meant a physical move too, to another section of the Ypres Salient, south of the Menin Road. The move also brought a series of congratulatory remarks, addressed to the battalions in the Division: on 7 August, the XVIII Corps Commander visited and thanked all the units in the 116th Brigade and two days later the Divisional Commander visited the Brigade and congratulated all units on their achievements.

That night the 11th Royal Sussex moved to excellent billets on the outskirts of Meteren, a short distance west of Bailleul; here Blunden appreciated the village church tower which 'serenely faced, along the stone road, the beautiful Moorish turrets of Bailleul Church'. (Perhaps the 'Moorish turrets' were a reminder of the Spanish occupation of the Low Countries in past centuries.) While they were here General Plumer visited their Brigade, now part of his Second Army. For the first time they had an American element amongst their number, for Lieutenant Worcester of the United States Medical Services took over from the battalion medical officer, who had gone on leave.

On his return from leave Blunden was promptly sent on a course at the Second Army Wireless School at Zuytpeene, west of Cassel. While stationed here he visited Cassel, where he met Lieutenant E. X. Kapp who had left the battalion on 1 June 1916, when they were both at Cuinchy, to become a 3rd Class Intelligence Officer. Kapp was now serving with the Army Press Bureau, an appointment which provided the luxury of living in châteaux and using army cars.

Ten days later Blunden was back with the battalion, from where, since Colonel Millward did not want him for the coming tour in the line, he was sent to the transport lines at Rozenhill, near Reninghelst. His friend Lieutenant Maycock was Transport Officer here and made use of Blunden as his assistant; here too he again took over the writing-up of the battalion War Diary. It was a complex and confusing area:

Taking up the rations used to be almost a laughing matter -

not so now. Merely to find the way through the multiplying tracks and desperate obliteration of local identity would have been a problem; to get horses and vehicles through, in the foundering night of dazzling wildfire and sweltering darkness, with shells coming and going in enormous shocks and gnashing ferocity, to the ration or working party crouching by some old shelters, was the problem. [U/W, p.211]

On 18 September the battalion was holding the line in Shrewsbury Forest when during the afternoon relief by the 17th K.R.R.C. (117th Brigade), a shell burst on a sap exit. Other Rank casualties included sergeants of the sniping and gas platoons and one from the Regimental Police, all of whom were killed. One of these was Sergeant Clifford, a well-respected battalion N.C.O. whose death caused Blunden personal sadness. The relief under way at the time of the hit was only partial,

Captain Geoffrey Salter MC (front row, fourth from left) with officers and senior NCOs of his company in 1917, (Note the two wound stripes on his sleeve.) Edmund Blunden has written in several names. Captain Salter had the terrible task of burying his brother Francis on the battlefield near Stuff Trench in October 1916. The officer on the front row, extreme right, is Second Lieutenant W R Botting, who was 'Severely Censured' as a result of trial by FGCM at Ypres in June 1917.

since Blunden's friend Captain Geoffrey Salter and two hundred men had been left in the line to act as prisoners' guard and stretcher bearers for the forthcoming operations.

With the exception of Captain Salter and his men, the battalion was fortunate in being excluded from the forthcoming operations. The 11th Royal Sussex was one of the many elements of the Second Army in its task to extend its left flank northwards by attacking the whole of the high ground crossed by the Menin Road. This would clearly not be easy, for the new elastic form of German defence - with lightly-held forward trench lines - tended to disorganise the attacking British force. The bulk of the enemy forces was kept in close reserve, ready to counter-attack before the British troops had time to consolidate on captured ground.

The 39th Division (Second Army) was near the farthest right end of a front that stretched over eight miles. The Second Army, together with the Fifth Army further north towards Langemarck, was to go into attack on 20 September 1917; the 39th Division main attacks were to be undertaken by the 117th and 118th brigades with the 116th (which included the 11th Royal Sussex) in reserve. Apart from the Tower Hamlets section, the battle was successful in overall terms: on 22 September Blunden wrote in the battalion War Diary that the two hundred men required for prisoners' guard had returned in safety, although the rest of the 39th Division had been less fortunate, suffering casualties of 47 officers and 929 men.

On 23 September the battalion was in the front line once more, at Clonmel Copse (south of the Menin Road, east of Sanctuary Wood), and moved next day to the Tower Hamlets sector. Two days later a German attack successfully penetrated the ground next to the 11th Sussex's left flank. Blunden, writing up the War Diary and describing swift and effective action by his friend Captain P. L. Clark, employed his usual elegant style in contrast with the terse entries that were the normality for these documents of record:

> But Captain Clark counter attacked on our own front to give the enemy no chance, running out into No Man's Land to meet him, after which he safeguarded our left flank by clearing the Germans from a dugout on the road. Our front therefore remained intact.

After about ten days in the Transport Lines, Blunden was suddenly recalled to rejoin the battalion HQ in the line, in front of Tower Hamlets. On 26 September the battalion attacked some buildings on the Gheluvelt road, as part of the 116th Brigade attack recorded by

TROOPS AT YPRES

PHOTO ANTONY d'YPRES 210719·16

The Labour Corps takes Ypres

From Blunden's album, 'The Labour Corps takes Ypres'. The ruined building in the background is the old Templars' Hall, Ypres' pre-war post office.

Blunden in the War Diary as wholly successful, taking all its objectives despite intense shelling.

Next came a distressing day at the two pillboxes which formed battalion headquarters, one used by the adjutant, his clerks and messengers and the doctor, and the other, thirty yards away, by Blunden, his signallers, and other men. Since they were originally German dugouts, the doors faced the German lines, but Blunden's at least had a 'concrete portico' to shield it. They suffered tremendous shelling, 'guns of all calibres pouring their fury into our small area' and the trenches around were full of bodies. The Aid-Post was hit and the doctor continued to work furiously. A runner called in at Blunden's post, then went back to the other one: someone reported an incident at their neighbouring headquarters, and when Shearing (Blunden's servant) returned from investigating he 'hurried back, wild-eyed, straining: 'Don't go over, sir: it's awful. A shell came into the door.' The doctor, Captain Gatchell, and all those with him were killed, including the runner.

Blunden duly wrote up the incident in the War Diary. As they moved back via Dumbarton Lakes to Bodmin Copse when relieved by the 13th Bn. Rifle Brigade, he closed the month's entries in the War Diary with 'Estimated casualties of last tour 10 Officers and 195 O.R.' In

HONOUR TO THE BRAVE!

Pte. W. E. SHEARING, 11th Battalion R. Sussex Regiment,

Who was awarded the Military Medal for most conspicuous gallantry and devotion to duty in the operations at Menin Road on the 25th, 26th and 27th September.

Throughout the intense shelling the Battalion experienced in the above mentioned operations, he many times carried stretchers, rations and messages. He also undertook, when there was a shortage of water, to find water and carry it up to the Battalion. He also helped the Signallers to run out their lines under heavy shelling. All this work he did voluntarily. He showed a notable contempt of danger, and an unflagging energy, and set an inspiring example to all that were with him.

"Honour to the Brave!', Private W E Shearing. Shearing, Blunden's orderly, won the Military Medal when the battalion was in action in the Tower Hamlets Sector. Note EB's pencilled addition to the citation, 'with Worley'.

Undertones of War he remarks that, 'We were supposed to have been making advances on this front too' (he found English poetry an enormous comfort at such a time, reading Edward Young's mid eighteenth-century poem 'Night Thoughts on Life, Death and Immortality').

'The Welcome'. In his poem about the incident in the pill-box, Blunden characteristically concentrates on banal detail and the depressing prevailing atmosphere; the red-headed adjutant proposes meeting for dinner and gets a sour response, while an officer just back from leave was pale and nervous:

Past war had long preyed on his nature,
And war had doubled in horror since.

The shell-burst is merely *'Something happened at Headquarters pillbox'* and the fact of six deaths is presented obliquely (*'There were six men in that concrete doorway,/Now a black muckheap blocked the way.'*). He makes it clear that the witnesses would never forget the event - almost a confession of how it affected him as a twenty-year-old observer and as a poet writing about it for publication seven years later in *Undertones of War.*

The battalion was due to spend fourteen days in tented accommodation in a farmyard near Mount Kokereele ('a noble highland'), for reorganisation, inspections and training. Despite wet weather, there was fine scenery to enjoy amidst the distractions; in

what was the greatest moment of any rest in Flanders for some of us, a sudden break in the clouds one morning revealed as in some marvellous lens a vast extent of the country southwards, towered cities and silver rivers, master-highways, blue church-spires, a broad and calm plain, until pyramidal shapes in the extreme distance were identifiable as the great slag-heaps in the Lens and Béthune coalfield. [U/W, p.220]

The images Blunden creates are like the landscape of some calm Dutch painting, a visual and mental escape from the actuality.

A short list of officer promotions which came through on 4 October 1917, as recorded by Blunden in the War Diary, included two of his particular friends - Limbery-Buse and Arnold Vidler, who both now became full Lieutenants. Two days later Colonel Millward, as C.O., told Blunden that he had been recommended for promotion to Captain, but that Brigadier-General Hornby would not hear of it. The excuse given was that Blunden was too young, but Blunden himself felt 'My offences against propriety of speech and demeanour were in any case

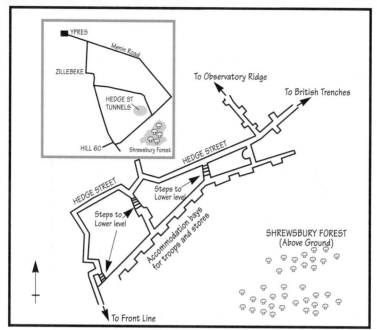

Sketch, part of the underground shelters known as the Hedge Street Tunnels. Blunden was Town Major in charge of this complex in October 1917 – an appointment carrying considerable power since it involved the allocation of comparatively safe billets in the dug-outs below ground. Those excluded were liable to suffer greater casualties, and senior officers were known to try to 'pull rank' to obtain the safer accommodation for their units.

sufficient to spoil my chances'. On 14 October, however, he was given a special duty: to be Town Major in Hedge Street Tunnels, near Observatory Ridge and close to Shrewsbury Wood. This involved allocating and regulating the very limited and highly coveted accommodation in the tunnels. In many ways it was a vital job; reasonably safe cover was limited and had to be carefully managed to avoid chaos and conflicting claims of priority for the scarce facilities. It was therefore a position of some power, although in an unhappy location.

To get there, however, meant moving from Zillebeeke to the dreaded Valley Cottages, from past experience a dangerous journey that he had never enjoyed - and in addition, on his way up to the position he found himself in the midst of a very heavy German barrage which lasted for an hour. It was typical of the circumstances that the dead body of a senior NCO remained in the entrance of a large dugout because it was too dangerous to spend even a short amount of time on burying the dead. Despite the dangers, however, men of the 13th Glosters - the Divisional Pioneers - were busy laying down wooden trolley-lines; but it seemed that as fast as they laid the new lines, enemy gunfire destroyed them.

Living conditions inside the tunnels were dirty and wretched - but safe, despite shell-fire that pounded the roof overhead from time to time. The main problem for Blunden was that more senior officers were tempted to try to usurp his authority as a mere subaltern; on one occasion a major in the Machine Gun Corps became quite objectionable while attempting to override Blunden's orders - but when Brigadier-General Hornby provided a signed paper indicating that young Blunden's word was law, the problems vanished and officers senior to him became more sympathetic.

Although not considered suitable for a captaincy, the normal rank for a Company Commander, Blunden was placed in command of 'B' Company when they arrived in the tunnels for a spell in the line in the 'River Hamlets Right Sector'. His entry in the War Diary for 16 October records that he had the battalion busily occupied in 'cleaning tunnels, building latrines, rearranging accommodation and burying the dead'. The last entry for the day reads laconically 'Enemy quiet (for this sector)'.

By 18 October the battalion was established in the line, in front of

Four views around Ypres, from Edmund Blunden's album.

Unfinished German "pillbox"

Gheluvelt: one of our objectives, 1917

Shellburst near Zillebeke Lake

Lingering look of Gheluvelt before war

Bodmin Copse and south of Tower Hamlets. Somewhat apprehensive, as this was not their usual sector, they began their four-day tour. Holding the line was by no means a quiet task: there was constant artillery fire, and mustard gas shells fell on at least two occasions, while at another time an enemy plane dropped bombs near battalion HQ and the front line.

Blunden's friend Arnold Vidler had 'a liking for No Man's Land', and on 19 October the two men went out to explore the area; they returned without incident, but soon after this the incoming 17th King's Royal Rifle Corps came under machine-gun fire in the same place. A patrol brought in two young Germans, who had been sitting there for many hours waiting for a target to fire on.

Blunden and his fellow Company Commanders occupied what they called 'Hunwater' dugout. It was so battered and derelict amongst the shattered huts and tree-stumps that for a while its occupation passed unnoticed. Unfortunately it came to enemy notice when Blunden's company halted briefly there just as German illuminating fire went up: correct drill required everyone to remain absolutely still, to avoid catching the watching enemy eye - but in this case one or two men, new to the war or nervous, betrayed the company's position by moving. Immediate machine gun fire was the consequence, and further illumination; but fortunately no supporting enemy artillery joined in, and after a short and no doubt uncomfortable wait in brightly-lit immobility they were able to go on their way unharmed. In due course Blunden and his men moved out of the Salient to the camp near Vierstraat which Blunden had recently reconnoitred [U/W, p.226].

In a letter to his young friend still at Christ's Hospital, Hector Buck, dated 23 October 1917, Blunden signs himself 'Napoleon Buonaparte', and also as Acting Adjutant. Written with all the free-and-easy confidence of old school friendship, the letter includes a vivid and humorous description of the dugout that he shared with his fellow company commanders. Writing the letter must have been a relief after his necessarily restrained notes in the War Diary:

> *In spite of all things let us be cheerful! The tents flap wildly in the teeth of the nor-easter, the mud stretches unimaginably that way and this, stolchy and skin-deep ... We string along the becrumped duckwalks in a darkness that may be felt, a remnant manages to find its way up to the foremost shellholes and lies down in them. The previous tenants quit as fast as the sludge will allow, and trust to God the S.O.S. won't go up before they get down past the guns; meantime the scorbutic Blunden is crawling*

around trying to find the ruins of Potiphar Farm or Usedtobe
Castle in order to get his correct dispositions back to a Fuming
and nail-nibbling C.O. ...

... there is no means of getting into the dugout except this
doorway, screened though it be with two or three ground sheets
and some German equipment: and once inside, the unguarded
foot suddenly falls lovingly into about 18 inches of Hunwater,
with noisome bubbles winking at the brim...the air is quite
devoid of oxygen, and the candle's light is not of this world. At
times, the snores of the sleeper drown the glutinous gurglings of
the Hunwater - or the arrival of a muster of 5.9's just outside the
door causes the last drain of whisky to jolt off the pro-table and
vanish for ever in the seething depths. And then up comes some
paper warfare - 'You will submit a Raid Scheme' or 'SECRET,
The Battalion will not be relieved for 25 years' or 'The 333rd
course for intending Landscape Painters will assemble at
Medicine Hat on the 1st April 1918. Coys. will detail 50 young
and intelligent men each, with if possible some knowledge of
wombat culture, gingernut-fancying and love cages, to report at
Bn HQ at 2 a.m. today. Rations for 1920 will be carried and the
men will have a bath before they leave the front line. (Sd)
Napoleon Buonaparte'

The battalion left the front and marched to Bois camp, about 200 yards
south-east of the Brasserie and near the wood of Bois Carré, close to
Vierstraat. After a bath session at Kemmel Château on 21 October (no
doubt extremely welcome), they moved on via Kemmel and Locre to
Carnarvon camp near Reninghelst. It had previously been used as
horse-lines, and was in a disgusting state: protests brought a further
move after four days, to Chippewa camp south-east of Zevekote, where
hutted billets were available. The War Diary entry for 31 October (in
Blunden's handwriting) reads:

Most of the men who came out with the battalion in March
1916 and were still with it were now enabled to get their leave.

While here, Blunden was instructed to make preparations for the
battalion to carry out some trench digging near Larch Wood. On 1
November 1917 it was his twenty-first birthday: an unpromising place
for such a celebration, and with what memories of the past twelve
months! But he was fortunate enough to have Sergeant Worley as his
companion on a reconnaissance outing near Larch Wood. It was a
dangerous spot, east of the Ypres - Comines railway - and not far from
the shattered village of Verbrandenmolen, 'a prominence crossed by

wooden roads and littered with slimed breakages'. As they passed through these ruins, enemy guns opened fire on the British artillery there, a German shell dropped on the plank roadway between the two Royal Sussex men and a Royal Engineers soldier just ahead: amazingly and fortunately, it failed to explode. Once inside the magnificently engineered Larch Wood Tunnels, in use as a medical headquarters, they were reasonably safe - unlike those working outside. South of Larch Wood, a deep railway cutting led to the notorious Hill 60, with its huge mine crater.

Blunden supervised the battalion as they carried out their digging duties, with very few casualties - although Worley was wounded in the leg ('he regarded this as an insult rather than injury, and hobbled on') - and then made his way back via Manor Farm to Shrapnel Corner, south of Ypres. While the new twenty-one-year-old was busy with arrangements for the battalion concert, he learned from a new doctor, an American - Captain Crassweller - that he would be departing for a two-month signalling course. While away he missed the news of the award of the prestigious Distinguished Conduct Medal to Sergeant Worley.

American medical officers with the British Army. The U.S.A. entered the war on the side of the Allies in April 1917. At that time its army was tiny but, determined to help, it sent over some hundreds of doctors who had either been drafted or had volunteered to serve in the U.S. Army Medical Corps Reserve. Much to their surprise, these men found that despite being commissioned officers in the U.S. Army they were now to serve in the British Army's RAMC, in many cases as battalion medical officers. The British practice of having medical officers near the front line had led to heavy losses since 1914, and this shortage could now be made good with the American arrivals. Blunden's battalion was one of the units which welcomed these well-qualified former hospital doctors.

Lieutenant Bernard Gallagher, U.S. Army Medical Corps, from Minnesota. He enlisted in the U.S. Army in April 1917 and was attached to the RAMC. He was eventually captured in the March 1918 retreat whilst serving with the 2/5th Glosters. The photograph was taken whilst he was in a German POW camp.

Blunden was not alone in leaving the battalion at this time: the next day, two officers received the welcome news that they were to leave immediately for England, for a six-months' instructor course. One of these was Blunden's friend from his schooldays, Arnold Vidler, now promoted to Captain, and the second was Captain G. Salter - he who at the capture of Stuff Trench overlooking the Ancre valley had had the painful task of burying his brother Francis.

The Army Signal School was located near Mont des Cats, about two miles from the famous monastery and half-way between Poperinghe to the north and Bailleul to the south. Blunden remarks that

> *Probably the underlying cause of the numberless 'schools' in the B.E.F. at this time was as much the desire to give officers and men a rest as to instruct them.*

During his two months at the Signalling School the active war was to see some significant events. Haig had decided to end the battles of Ypres; Gough's Fifth Army, no longer needed in the Salient, moved south to the Amiens area by 14 November, and a week later Byng's Third Army opened operations at Cambrai. This was a brilliant surprise attack, but failed to make significant gains and ended by the beginning of December. Next, the Fifth Army took over VII Corps where their three-division front was on the right of the Third Army, stretching

Christmas 1917. Blunden at the Signal School at the Mont des Cats (back row far right), and a modern view of the exterior wall, showing plaques that commemorate the Canadian presence here in the First World War.

southwards from Gouzeaucourt to Roisel, east of Péronne. The 39th Division, including Blunden's 11th Royal Sussex, would be required to leave the Ypres area and join VII Corps at Gouzeaucourt.

His signalling course ended, Blunden returned to his battalion on 11 January 1918. It was by now encamped near Irish Farm, north of St. Jean (Sint Jan), near the point where the 11th Royal Sussex had formed up for the Brigade attack on St Julien on 31 July 1917; Blunden and his friend Second Lieutenant Olive decided to explore, and see what they could recognise. The scene was very different now, with the roads drained and the area full of Nissen huts. This work, undertaken by the 39th Divisional Pioneers, in the form of the 13th Bn Gloucestershire Regiment, had had its human cost - 300 casualties suffered in the five month period of their activities - and this by a battalion ostensibly there in a non-fighting capacity.

The press and the army

There was a constant rumble of discontent concerning the inaccuracy of military actions as described in newspaper accounts. Blunden recounts a typical incident at the Signalling School:

We also went to a lecture by a war correspondent, who invited questions, whereon a swarthy old colonel rose and said, 'The other day I was obliged to take part in a battle. I afterwards read a war correspondent's account of the battle, which proved to me that I hadn't been there at all. Will the lecturer explain that, please?' [U/W, p.235]

Visit: Take the Menin Road towards Hooge, passing the Hooge Crater Cemetery on the right and museum on the left, then two monuments at 'Clapham Junction' - to the 18th Division on the right and the Gloucesters on the left. At the first crossroads, 100 yards beyond the edge of the wood, turn right before the village sign 'Geluveld'. Go straight ahead for about a quarter of a mile, over a very minor crossroads: you are now in the 'Tower Hamlets' area where Blunden was in action in September 1917.

Reverse direction and return to the minor crossroads; turn left into s'Henrenthage Straat, and left again at the T-junction into Pappotstraat. Carry on to a fork in the road, identifiable from the tree in the road island, and bear right (signposted 'Zillebeke') into Zandvoordestraat. 'Shrewsbury Forest' is on the left here. Immediately on the left is the site of Hedge Street Tunnels, where Blunden acted as Town Major. Continue for about 200 yards (through the area known as Observatory Ridge), and a house comes into view on the left, which is on the site of Rudkin House. As the road runs down from Observatory Ridge it winds

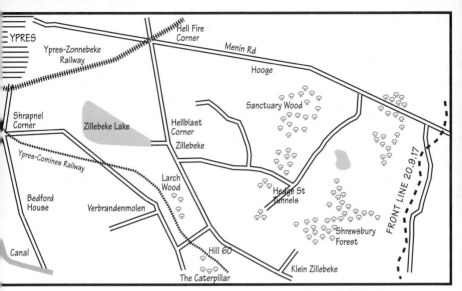

The Ypres Salient – south-east of Ypres, to illustrate the visit. Blunden
served on this front at various times during 1917.

between modern houses; at and beyond the Zillebeke village marker on
the right of the road was the site of Blunden's 'dreaded' Valley Cottages,
where RSM Daniels was fatally wounded at battalion HQ.

Turn left at the T-junction into Wervikse Straat and continue up the
hill to Zwartleen. Turn right at the top into Zwarteleenstraat and Hill 60
comes into view (marked by a 'Hill 60' sign). Cross over the railway, then
turn right at the T-junction on to the Verbrandenmolen road
(Komenseweg). Blunden was here in November 1917 with Sgt. Worley,
coming under German artillery fire which was directed at some large
calibre guns. One of the German shells dropped on the roadway just
ahead of them as they were making their way to tunnels in Larch Wood
about 400 yards away beyond the railway, but fortunately failed to
explode. Larch Wood (Railway Cutting) cemetery is near the site today.

Continue, and at the next right turn cross over the railway (level
crossing) into Blawe Poort Straat, Zillebeke. In the village, turn left into
Maal Destede Straat and stop outside the church. The village
churchyard is sometimes known as 'the aristocrats' cemetery', a name
easily understood by reading the British headstones. Blunden passed
the church several times as Brigade Intelligence Officer, accompanied
by his corporal observer.

Walk up the street, leaving the church on your right, and turn down
the path signposted In't Riet CC, a few yards away on the left beside a
small stream. This was known to the British as 'Hellblast Corner'.
Further along the path, Zillebeke Lake comes into view - this was the
track used by Blunden on his way from Ypres to the front line when he
was Intelligence Officer. (A modern cycle/footpath leads to Ypres.)

Zillebeke churchyard, 'the aristocrats' cemetery'. Blunden passed the churchyard in March 1917 and noticed the wooden crosses in it. These would have marked the graves of members of the Guards and Household Cavalry killed in November 1914 at Shrewsbury Forest.

Return to the car, continue up the hill to the Menin road at Hellfire Corner, and turn left for Ypres.

By chance, it was Blunden's turn to go on leave, and he was the butt of some condescending and jocular remarks by the major who was in temporary command of the battalion. The suggestion was that, following several weeks away from active duty at an army school,

Blunden in Ypres: two views of his poem 'Can you remember?' displayed on the ramparts, close to the Menin Gate.

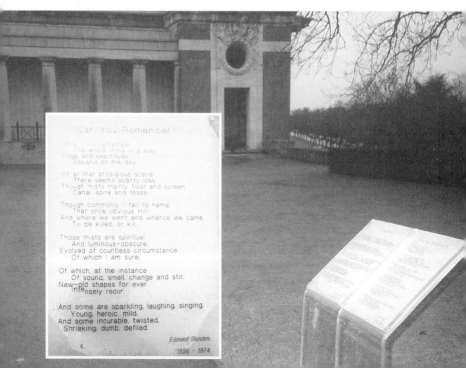

Blunden should perhaps feel it appropriate to forego his leave. Blunden, who for some reason had taken a strong dislike to this officer, pointed out that it had not been his wish to go the Signals School, and he intended to take his leave entitlement [U/W, p.235]. His wishes - and rights - prevailed, and two days later (13 January 1918) he left for England, together with his American medical friend Captain Crassweller.

The acting C.O. who objected to Blunden's leave was Major H. S. Lewis. As a lieutenant in the battalion before Blunden's arrival he had won a Military Cross at Givenchy on 27 March 1916, and was wounded at the Boar's Head, near Port Arthur, on 30 June 1916. On 1 March 1917, when Colonel Harrison returned to England, Lieutenant Lewis took over from Major Millward, the new C.O., as Second in Command of the battalion in the front line on Observatory Ridge, but a week later Captain A. G. L. Owen returned to duty and took over again from Lewis.

By the end of the month, March 1917, Lewis was battalion adjutant and by August he held the rank of Captain and acted as 2 i/c from time to time. By mid-December he was a major, and in Colonel Millward's absence on leave that month he was Acting Commanding Officer. He was clearly a competent and effective officer, and although the cause of Blunden's dislike for him is not known, it may have been the result of some purely personal antipathy. Blunden's youth and quick sensibilities must have frequently brought him into unspoken conflict with others - perhaps too his observant eye and the precision of his words may have been less than popular with his fellow-officers if he felt inclined to air his views a little too freely. There are hints of several arguments in *Undertones of War* - but it is hard to imagine how disagreements could have been avoided in the generally prevailing conditions.

The battalion had welcomed their orders to leave the Salient, for after more than a year around Ypres it was a relief to look forward to fresh surroundings. They headed south and joined VII Corps, part of Sir Hubert Gough's Fifth Army.

This enthusiasm did not last long. Having paused at Cerisy-Gailly on their way, on 30 January 1918 they marched to Corbie for a four-hour train journey to Péronne, followed by another two hours' march early next day, to a tented camp near Mont St. Quentin outside Péronne. Next day they moved on again, to the Forward Area near Gouzeaucourt, and relieved the 12th Royal Scots in Reserve at

137

Mont St Quentin, near Péronne, the view today from the west. The 11th Royal Sussex marched through here on 31 January 1918, on their way to Gouzeaucourt. Blunden, on his way back from leave in England, arrived here a few days later and stayed in a hutted camp before catching up with his battalion.

Revelon Farm.

The surrounding countryside, undulating and dotted with ruined villages and copses, showed all too clearly the devastation left by the German troops as they dynamited orchards, churches and bridges during their withdrawal in 1917 to the Hindenburg Line. The forward zone under the Fifth Army consisted of a continuous line of front, with strong points in Gauche Wood and Quentin Redoubt.

The land was well wired, with designated anti-tank areas. Revelon Farm, prominently set on a ridge between Heudicourt and Gouzeaucourt, had strong defences and was fully garrisoned: battalions out of the line were stationed here in reserve. The front line was about 1½ miles to the east of the farm, with the British and German lines well separated, and at first the newly-arrived units found it an almost suspiciously quiet posting: the wariness was well-founded, for the German army was preparing for its devasting offensive in the spring of 1918 which would push the British back for as much as forty miles in some places.

Rejoining the battalion after his leave, Blunden found changes: as part of a general reduction in brigade size, the 12th Royal Sussex had been disbanded, and ten of its officers and 200 Other Ranks joined the 11th Royal Sussex in February 1918. The brigade now consisted of the 11th and 13th Royal Sussex, and the 14th Hampshires.

The whole area had been involved in the Battle of Cambrai in November-December 1917, and was littered with relics, including destroyed and abandoned tanks around Gouzeaucourt. Gauche Wood was full of weaponry left over after a combined tank, infantry and cavalry attack on 1 December, but much of it was being salvaged and a light railway (operated by U.S. Army engineers) transported it to Heudicourt [U/W, p. 239]. The front line was very different from life around Ypres or Thiepval, for during a spell in the trenches Blunden was able to sit on the trench parapet and look at the distant German lines; he noted the ruins of Villers-Ghislain and its large cemetery, apparently without endangering himself.

These comparatively relaxed conditions were confirmed when, on 12 February, the whole brigade together with Divisonal Pioneers and parties of Royal Engineers was engaged in putting out barbed wire in No Man's Land, a formidable task demanding silence to escape unwelcome enemy attention. With such large numbers, noise was inevitable but - possibly because of the width of land between the opposing front lines - the British wiring parties were able to finish their operations before the German machine-guns opened fire.

It was around this time that Blunden, fresh from the Signalling

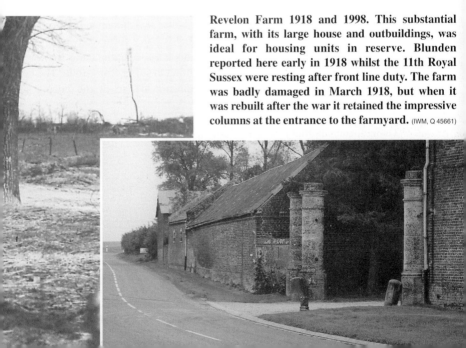

Revelon Farm 1918 and 1998. This substantial farm, with its large house and outbuildings, was ideal for housing units in reserve. Blunden reported here early in 1918 whilst the 11th Royal Sussex were resting after front line duty. The farm was badly damaged in March 1918, but when it was rebuilt after the war it retained the impressive columns at the entrance to the farmyard. (IWM, Q 45661)

Gauche Wood and Villers-Ghislain cemetery, 1999. In 1918 the British lines ran through Gauche Wood; early in the year Blunden looked across from the trench parapet beside the wood, and observed this cemetery and the ruins of Villers-Ghislain. No Man's Land was quite wide here.

course, tried out his new skills. This involved climbing a tree in Gauche Wood and attempting signal-lamp flashes to Battalion HQ - but he mistook the direction, his efforts were spotted by the enemy, and machine-gun fire opened up into the wood. Despite this minor mishap, he was appointed Adjutant on 14 February, which was also the date of a battalion visit by Lieutenant-General Sir William Congreve, VC.

Although Blunden had escaped unwanted enemy attention when observing No Man's Land, a more senior officer was less fortunate: this was Brigadier-General Hornby, who was spotted when he mounted the fire step on a front-line trench visit. Blunden suggested he step down, which he did, recognising the young officer by name - no doubt remembering him from Blunden's fairly lengthy period of working for him, which was possibly made more memorable by less than diplomatic behaviour.

On 21 February 1918 Blunden handed over as Adjutant and left for England 'for six months' rest'. He felt that it was a form of treachery to return to the safety of England while his friends continued to fight, although he recognised that he was beginning to suffer from strain. The feeling of abandoning his comrades appears in one of the poems included in *Undertones of War*:

Gouzeaucourt military cemetery, looking towards Villers-Ghislain.

He was sent to an army training camp in Suffolk, where he was clearly
not happy: there was an uncomfortable atmosphere between those who
had seen active service in the war and those who had not. Blunden
applied to return to the 11th Royal Sussex, but was refused as 'unfit'.
After the Armistice, and by now married to a Suffolk girl, he returned
to France, but in February 1919 demobilisation was on offer and he
returned to an unpredictable civilian life.

Beyond the Armistice

Life in the battalion continued calmly after Blunden's departure in
February 1918 as it carried on with its regular rhythm. Blunden's duties
as Adjutant were taken over by his friend, Lieutenant and
Quartermaster B. F. Swain, and at the end of the month another friend,
Lieutenant Limbery-Buse - like Blunden himself - was posted back to
England for six months' rest.

Gradually artillery came into action in both front lines, and German
aircraft were active overhead. When the great German advance came
in 21 March 1918 the 11th Royal Sussex were in reserve, but were
quickly involved in the fighting round Villers-Faucon to the south of
Gouzeaucourt and the withdrawal towards Péronne. They crossed the
River Somme at Buscourt, continued to Hem-Monacu on 24 March
and then across the Roman St-Quentin - Amiens road to Harbonnières,
which they reached on 28 March 1918.

They made at stand on 29 March near Villers-Bretonneux, near the
extensive and important sidings at Marcelcave on the main Amiens -
Ham railway line, but their retreat continued. Two days later they were
at Hangard Wood, and here troops of 18th Division took over. The

Drawn by I. Meo at
GOUZEAUCOURT, March 1918

[His daughter Anne Innes Meo came to see us at Long Melford on 7 Nov. 1964; he is still living, aged nearly 80. He was made a prisoner of war soon after he drew this.

'My latest ordeal. When will it End?!!!' Edmund Blunden's album, pencil sketch of Gouzeaucourt, March 1918.

battalion could not know it at the time, but the Fifth Army's retreat was almost over. By 4 April the line was re-established on the Cachy - Villers-Bretonneux road: the Germans had been stopped a mere nine miles short of Amiens and, to quote Ludendorff, 'the enemy's resistance was beyond our powers'.

Battalion casualties came to 320 officers and men, some of them recorded missing but actually taken prisoner, including seven officers (out of twenty absent at roll call) captured during the long retreat. This included two Company commanders. One of the three officers killed in action at this time was Lieutenant/Quartermaster Swain, who had taken over from Blunden as the battalion Adjutant. As with so many, his grave was overrun and lost on the retreat, and he is commemorated on the Pozières memorial. Safe in camp in England, Blunden must have searched anxiously for information on friends and colleagues. News of the wounding on 23 March of Brigadier-General Hornby, on whose staff he had served, must surely have reached him. The depleted ranks of the 11th Royal Sussex eventually reached St Omer on 9 April.

The battalion had not quite finished with the war, for they were soon back in the Ypres Salient, attacking and digging trenches to repel German attacks. Eventually it was divided, with part acting as instructors to the American forces, and in June 1918 it was back in England and taking in men from a battalion of the Queen's Own Royal West Kent Regiment in preparation for a new assignment. On 17 October it left Scotland for the campaign in North Russia, just over four years from its formation in Bexhill in 1914.

Notes & Sources
The Cellars of Marcelcave, A Yank Doctor in the BEF, C. J. Gallagher, Burd Street Press, 1998

Sketch map of the movements of the 11th Royal Sussex after Blunden's departure. He left them just before the German offensive of March 1918; this map shows their route during its fighting retreat to Hangard Wood.

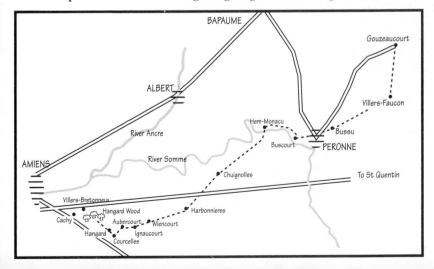

Chapter Seven

1918 AND THE END OF THE WAR

**'The old Great War ended, and one trouble that followed
was that Peace was not all happiness'**
Edmund Blunden, (*War Poets 1914-1918,* 1958)

If there had been no war, the young scholar Edmund Blunden would
have moved straight from one notable teaching establishment - Christ's
Hospital - to another, Oxford, to take up his Classics scholarship; and
then what? teaching, perhaps (taking after his parents); writing, surely
poetry, a life in academia, of literary exploration and practice.

These of course were what he did engage in, for the rest of his life
after the war: but the life, the writing and the feelings were changed
from the might-have-been by the overwhelming experiences of the war
years. Much of *Undertones of War* is concerned with the individuals
who shared his war with him, and these concerns - with the war, with
the rural landscapes in which he grew up and in which he fought, above
all with the people who shared them with him and who he grew to love

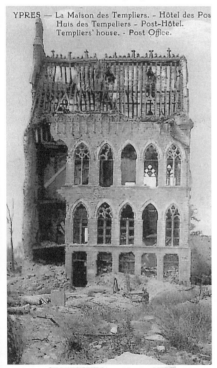

YPRES — La Maison des Templiers. - Hôtel des Pos
Huis des Tempeliers - Post-Hôtel.
Templiers' house. - Post Office.

? final
ruin

- can be seen throughout his writing.
His poetry adds images, insights and
intricate layers of observation and
feeling for the reader to tease out, for
the indications are often subtle and
indirect. The thoughtful presentation
of his younger self make it hard to
remember just how young he was,
barely 22 when the war ended, his
maturity and adulthood hastened by
the forcing-ground of the trenches.

In February 1918 Blunden was
despatched to Suffolk for six months'
duty at a training centre near
Stowmarket: a relief in many ways, for
he was removed not only from the
constant danger but also from the day-
to-day strains and irritations, and
somewhat uncomfortable relationships
with his senior officers. Reading
between the lines, it seems likely that

**Ruins in Ypres: the old Templars' Hall,
the former Post Office, taken from
Edmund Blunden's album.**

the young officer with his quick mind and great expressive skill could be an uneasy presence under strain, inclined to give forceful expression to his feelings. Even ten years later, he was able to refer to the circumstances of war as crushing the soul out of eighteen-year-old boys.

It was during this period in England, however, that his life took an unexpected turn, for in Bury St Edmunds he met Mary Daines, a local girl from an unsophisticated and unliterary background. They were married in June 1918, when he was twenty-one and Mary only eighteen. Mary was one of a large and loving family, closely concerned with rural life (her father was a village blacksmith): her family, their essential part in rural life, and the confidence in future happiness and security that marriage represented, must have created a welcome harbour from the war.

Certainly, in *The Mind's Eye* (1934) he recorded great confusion in 1918 and the early part of 1919, concerning war and peace, the strangeness and loss of the structures into which he had been born and had grown up. As for so many returning veterans of any rank, the end of the war did not bring peace, and Blunden later remarked that he thought of his war experience every day for the rest of his life. It continued to invade his poetry, coloured his thoughts, too often his dreams, and shaped his writing and his philosophy. It was an essential framework for many friendships - running from his sergeant, Worley, to the much-admired Colonel Harrison.

A new and valued friend was Siegfried Sassoon, whose poems had provided one of the few rewarding moments around Ypres. In 1919 he wrote to the older man, who was by then literary editor of the Daily Herald, enclosing copies of his schoolboy poems that were about to be issued. Sassoon responded warmly, and helped Blunden with introductions in literary circles. It was the start of a lifelong friendship, with the added dimension of a shared passion for cricket.

Domestic life, despite its happy and hopeful start, did not provide enduring happiness: personal tragedy struck when in August 1919 the Blundens' first baby, Joy, died suddenly at the age of only five weeks - a sadness that did not fade. When his old school-friend Hector Buck visited the young couple two months later, he found them

> *physically and spiritually battered and exhausted ...* [Mary] *in the deepest mourning, him bowed, little, prematurely aged, shabbily dressed ...*

First for the young pair was Oxford, where Edmund took up his place at St John's College. As with school life and the army, the university became the source of valued friendships, not least with other young-old men whose student life was a return to academia after the disturbing world of the war. Student life soon took second place in his life, however, and in the summer of 1920 Blunden left Oxford and took up a part-time post with the *Athenaeum,* exercising what Sassoon called 'his aura of enthusiasm for literature' in working as 'office boy' for this distinguished literary magazine (and contributing to its pages). This useful step into the London literary world was achieved through the intervention of 'our kindest of friends', Lady Ottoline Morrell.

Literary Friendships. As Blunden's biographer Barry Webb notes, this group of undergraduate friends included some names that would become well known in the literary world - Edgell Rickword, L. A. G. Strong, Richard Hughes, Arthur Bryant, Charles Morgan, and others. Then there were Robert Nichols - friend of Robert Graves and Siegfried Sassoon - Graves and Sassoon themselves (though the friendship with Graves soon grew strained) and, further afield, Ottoline Morrell and her eclectic range of visitors.

In the course of his long life the name of Edmund Blunden was linked with many well-known names in English literature past and present: he identified strongly with John Clare, the poverty-stricken rural poet of the eighteenth century whose work Blunden presented to a modern readership in the 1920s, and in 1931 was responsible for a widely-read and influential edition of Wilfred Owen's poems. It is perhaps significant that both these poets suffered great mental distress and were unknown in their own lifetime: Blunden not only admired their writing deeply, he felt the need to bring them and their poetry to public attention, and worked hard to achieve this.

A significant change of direction came in 1924, when Blunden was appointed Professor of English Literature at the Imperial University of Tokyo. He travelled without his wife, for Mary could not face the thought of spending three years so far away - and arrived to scenes of physical destruction that must have reminded him of the war: less than a year earlier the great Tokyo earthquake of September 1923 had shattered buildings and killed more than 100,000 people. The new English professor had to move from one classroom to another, conditions were thoroughly uncomfortable, and the occasional window-shattering earth tremor reminded him of shells bursting along the Western Front. Lonely at first, he missed Mary and their two children Clare and John, but grew in time to appreciate the richness and beauties of Japanese culture. He achieved a great rapport with his students: a future generation of Japanese intellectuals was influenced by his attitudes and his teaching.

He lectured, prepared his lectures for publication, compiled an anthology of English poetry for his students and continued with journalism and poetry which was despatched to England. And as well as all this work for Japan and for home consumption, he wrote *Undertones of War*, aided only by one or two trench-maps and a few notes.

He returned to England in the summer of 1927 and picked up his active life of literary creation and journalism. Friendships were revived and Sassoon was a loyal supporter through some financial difficulties, but there was great sadness when after a

Yalding High Street from in front of Cleaves School, with the village war memorial in the foreground.

period of weary strain and unhappiness it became clear that his marriage had broken down. He and Mary were divorced in 1931.

This personal sadness contrasted with public acclaim, with the publication in 1928 of his greatest literary success - not the poems that were his most constant exercise, but his recollections of the war that had shaped his young adult years. *Undertones of War,* published in 1928 when he was 33, is the mature distillation of his younger self.

The opening and closing sentences of this autobiographical memoir are typical of Blunden's oblique approach, and are often quoted: the first words of Chapter One are 'I was not anxious to go' and the final chapter, 'My Luck', ends with a description of travelling across quiet and beautiful French countryside early in 1918, leaving the front line and returning to England. Unaware of the final savage burst of war ahead which would destroy so many men in the final months to November 1918, and without any foreboding about his own future, he describes himself as 'a harmless young shepherd in a soldier's coat'.

1930 was a year of literary success, with a biography (of 'Old Blue' Leigh Hunt) as well as *Undertones*, but overwork and his marriage breakdown undermined his health. He returned early next year to live with his parents in Yalding, the beloved landscape of his childhood. His

147

Edmund Blunden in the late 1940s.

main concern now was to edit the poems of Wilfred Owen, a task which Sassoon had turned down for himself because he felt too closely associated with his dead friend. It was a complex but rewarding task, and he was able to bring some personal insight to his lengthy introductory memoir, defining Owen as a war poet but not only of the war - he was 'a poet without classifications of war and peace'.

It was more than mere coincidence that saw Blunden editing the poems of Wilfred Owen for publication in 1931, with a lengthy memoir on Owen's life: he perceived Owen's attitude to the war as similar to his own, with the poetry as witness. (What a wonderful chance of history it would have been if Blunden and Owen could have met - but it was not until after the war that he encountered and appreciated the work of Owen, Edward Thomas, Gurney and Rosenberg; and although he visited Gurney in his asylum in Kent, Owen, Thomas and Rosenberg were all killed during the war.)

In the autumn of 1931 he returned to Oxford, where he became a don in Merton College. During the 1930s he taught, wrote, and looked for ways of avoiding future wars; up to the eve of the 1939 war he did his best to persuade the world that further conflict was not inevitable, that it should be avoided by any means possible. These efforts led to some political discomfort, since his concern became confused by others with 1930s appeasement.

Once war broke out in 1939, however, Blunden put aside his misgivings, and contributed in both military and personal terms: he served with Oxford University O.T.C. as a map instructor, and corresponded with students away in the forces (including perhaps the

best-known poet of the Second World War, Keith Douglas). As Europe came under threat again he looked back again to his 'own' war, and appealed to the memory of Wilfred Owen:

Would you were not dust.

With you I might invent, and make men try

Some genuine shelter from this frantic sky.

Listening to cricket; Edmund Blunden (left) with the radio between him and Siegfried Sassoon, at Sassoon's house in Wiltshire.

('To W.O. and His Kind', April 1939)

A year later he wrote to The Times, to protest against indiscriminate bombing of German cities, and came under suspicion for apparently 'pro-German' sentiments, to his great disgust.

> The depth of his personal feeling for other victims of war can be seen in his continuing correspondence with the mothers of two dead poets whose work he greatly admired (Wilfred Owen, killed in 1918 and Keith Douglas, killed in 1944) and of his 'Old Blue' friend Arnold Vidler. He regarded Vidler as equally a victim of the war, since his suicide in 1924 was a long-delayed reaction to his experiences with the 11th Royal Sussex and his brother's death in action.

In 1944 he resigned his post in Oxford and joined *The Times Literary Supplement*. Peace brought a return to his past, with a two-year spell in Japan as Cultural Liaison Officer with the British Mission at an important stage in post-war recovery. He received many honours here, with a Japanese professor recording that 'the greatest merits of the occupation period in Japan were the dispatch of General MacArthur from the United States and Professor Blunden from the United Kingdom'. It was a time of intensive work, teaching, discussing, travelling - and enjoying family life once more, for in 1945 he had married one of his former Oxford students, and his young wife and their growing family brought domestic happiness.

In 1950 Blunden returned once again to London and *The Times Literary Supplement*. By now in his mid-fifties, Edmund Blunden was a well-known poet and prolific literary figure, much in demand and as

Blunden in Japan; 'The President of Keio, Dr Ushioda, makes me an Honorary Professor, February 1915.'

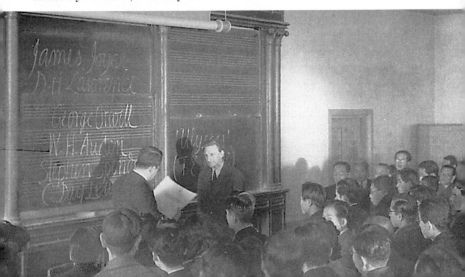

The Blunden family house in Long Melford and the plaque beside the gate, unveiled in 1996 during centenary celebrations.

wide in his interests as ever, which included editorial work for the Imperial [later Commonwealth] War Graves Commission.

Three years later, in September 1953, (nearly thirty years after his first period in Japan) the Blunden family travelled east again for Edmund to take up the post of Professor of English at the University of Hong Kong. It was an interesting but demanding post for a man in his late fifties with a young and lively family, and with much administration as well as teaching, and features of academic life such as dramatic productions and a constant stream of visitors to distract him from his own writing. He travelled widely, visiting Japan five times, undertook programmes of lectures and recordings, and explored mainland China, in particular its educational system. His diplomatic interest in the Communist regime was misconstrued on his return to Hong Kong and - having been attacked as pro-German in 1939 - he was now accused of being pro-Communist. The local press hostility blew over, however, and he revisited China again later.

This aspect of his far-eastern life must have provided a marked contrast with one of his visits to London when, in 1963, he attended a grand formal dinner to be made a Companion of Literature by the Royal Society of Literature, in the presence of more than a hundred literary figures (Edith Sitwell, Evelyn Waugh and Aldous Huxley were similarly honoured at the same dinner). In 1964, tired and with his memories of the First World War still a disturbing feature in his life, he returned to England and retired to Long Melford, in Suffolk.

Here he could enjoy literary friendships, contribute short items to *The Times Literary Supplement,* give lectures and enjoy village life. Memories of his young self, his trench life in France and around Ypres, drew him to Belgium and France several times - and his literary life took yet another turning when in 1966 he was elected as Oxford Professor of Poetry, a post of honour rather than academic burden. None the less, its demands and publicity were unwelcome, he fell ill and was haunted by the past. Important people were vanishing as death

150

claimed both Sassoon and his mother in 1967 (in her hundredth year, following his father many years earlier); Sgt. Worley already gone in 1954 (in his epitaph poem, Blunden wrote of him that *'There was no death but you would face it/Even in your youth'*), Colonel Harrison in 1964; his first wife Mary in 1956, his second wife Sylva in 1971. Mentally and physically he withdrew from life, and on 20 January 1974 he died peacefully at home.

In the churchyard of Long Melford's beautiful village church, his tombstone is engraved with lines from his poem 'Seers', set between the lines of his name and dates:

> *I live still, to love still*
> *Things quiet and unconcerned.*

As the coffin was committed to the ground, a wreath of Flanders poppies was dropped onto it by a figure from the past: Private A. E. Beeney, of the 11th Royal Sussex Regiment, who had been Edmund's runner at Ypres and Passchendaele.

Who was this man, whose life covered so many places, so many experiences? For the attentive reader, he tells us: his personality is there to be read, in his poems and in *Undertones of War*. In his delicately sketched portraits of people encountered, his eye that was both observant and psychologically perceptive, he expresses his feelings and impressions with a light touch that brings out personality, detail and incident. He knew that the war remained with him: in 1924, writing his 'Preliminary' to *Undertones of War* in Tokyo, he noted that 'I must go over the ground again'. Much later he remarked (in *The Poet Speaks*, 1966) that he always intended *Undertones of War* to be seen as:

The Blunden window in Yalding church – seen from the outside, and woodcut of the engraving. It was engraved in 1979 by Laurence Whistler, a friend of Blunden's, and shows a trench, barbed wire resembling living briar, and a shell-burst like a tree in blossom. The window also shows three stanzas from his poem 'Report on Experience'.

a sort of long poem. It varies, of course, in topics, but the uniting argument, if there is one, is that war is like that and ought not to happen.

Commentators on Blunden's life, in both biography and literary criticism, note the pervading insistence of the war in his work, even when he is ostensibly concerned with other matters - what has been described as 'war hauntedness'. The dedication to nature, to the rural past and the features of rural life, is intense - perhaps these familiar elements and certainties gave shape to his own life and helped to balance the continuing memory of the war years. Robyn Marsack remarks that

> *...allegiance to a specifically English tradition of nature poetry was in Blunden's case a source of strength. He derived his understated authority from the fact that rural subjects were for him inseparable from childhood ...*

> *...For Blunden pastoralism was not an empty academic form, it recreated the natural world he had intimately known.*

> *...The subtle interpenetration of human, non-human, and inanimate objects is one of the strengths of Blunden's war poetry.*

He possessed:

> *a perception of unyielding nature, that repels man's attempts at communion or description'*

Feeling for his natural surroundings was essential to his emotional security, but it was not a sentimental or easy refuge. In his poem 'Forefathers', published in 1922, he wrote of the untold earlier generations, utterly vanished, whose presence could just be guessed at from the landscape they had created, the few names recorded in a family Bible, and the houses, barns, mills they had built. The domestic landscape, created by man in collaboration with Nature, was his necessary framework and refuge, while the ruins and wastes of the battlefield were hostile: the glimpses of wildlife continuing within and around it were a comfort in the strains and dangers of the war.

Literary Echoes

All commentators note this constant presence of the war in Blunden's poetry, and that:

> *...this quality of passionate recollection set Blunden apart from the rural poets of his generation.*[1]

The same writer links him with Edward Thomas and Ivor Gurney. He comments that Blunden

> *...recognises that the war has made the retreat into*

1. Martin Taylor's 1996 edition of Blunden's war poems, *Overtones of War*, notes that the effect of the First World War affected 'not only his moral outlook but also his creative voice'. He also quotes Robyn Marsack's *Selected Poems*, that many of his poems are 'honeycombed with martial vocabulary and meaning'.

pastoralism no longer an adequate response' ...

and that

> *his war poems of this period are not based on any revolution*
> *in style, technique or attitude, as with Sassoon or Owen, but*
> *rather on an adaptation of pastoralism to his new experiences ...*
> *His ability to describe scenes of war through the eyes of a*
> *pastoral poet is the source of his emotional stability and his*
> *imaginative freedom. By adapting his poetry to his*
> *circumstances he was not overwhelmed by them. Instead he*
> *attains a balance both in language - when he describes the*
> *beauties of nature his phrasing is that of a pastoral poet; when*
> *he describes the effects of war his vocabulary reflects the*
> *violence of the scene - and sensibility - the power of pastoralism*
> *is diminished because the reality of war is overwhelming.*

Desmond Graham writes that:

> *We are not invited to absorb war into our ponderings but to*
> *see its recalcitrance; not invited to prize more highly the*
> *peaceful values which his poems cherish but to take those values*
> *as points of departure in an attempt to comprehend the wholly*
> *different experience of which he writes.*

Sassoon maintained that Blunden was the poet of the war most
lastingly obsessed by it. Unlike Sassoon's bitter and biting satires,
Blunden lets his unease, his perception and his close observations
creep quietly into the reader's mind almost surreptitiously - and the
reader wonders at the maturity forced upon this young and intellectual
officer. He writes of the moments away from the line, out of immediate
danger or action, but with the haunting knowledge of what awaits his
return to the front-line trenches, the implication sliding into his lines
almost between the words as it slides into the reader's mind almost
unnoticed. The deliberate concentration on Nature, the beauties and
tiny incidents of wild-life, become a support almost desperately
sought, an antidote to the murderous intensity and the energy-sapping
duration.

Blunden does not set out to persuade the reader one way or the other
- he is not a proselytiser: he records his own observations, of people,
places and incidents, then leaves the reader to discover through
attentive reading how these circumstances affected human flesh and
spirit. His touch is light but much more precise than it first appears:
behind the pastoral landscape, between the ruins and the trenches, the
true and most enduring damage (to feelings, beliefs, prospects) is
clearly visible. He often leaves the poem with a warning touch or a

note that demands thought, active engagement from the reader - so that the reader has to engage actively with the writer's mind and respond to his lines.

There are many poems that echo the war and personal experiences, often stating clearly that they are 'revisitations' - too many even to quote the titles here. Perhaps it is sufficient to refer to three, all included in *Undertones of War*: 'Third Ypres', published in 1922, was written in specific recollection of 'July 31, 1917 & the next day or two'. It describes the events and the atmosphere of 'the dreadful day', the incident when he is stunned by a shell landing on the pill-box, but where a tiny incident of wild-life at the scene helps to steady his mind:

> *O I'll drag you, friends,*
> *Out of this sepulchre into the light of day,*
> *For this is day, the pure and sacred day.*
> *And while I squeak and gibber over you,*
> *Look, from the wreck a score of field-mice nimble,*
> *And tame and curious look about them; (these*
> *Calmed me, on these depended my salvation).*

In 'Another Journey from Béthune to Cuinchy', written in the mid or late 1920s, he writes of seeing himself in 1916, walking by 'the green silent water'. He recalls the sights and sounds, the names (both local French and invented English), and expresses his confusion between then and now - 'Do you jib at my tenses? Who's who? you or I?' and continues the dialogue until, finally,

> *I see him walking*
> *In a golden-green ground,*
> *Where pinafored babies*
> *And skylarks abound,*
> *But that's his own business.*
> *My time for trench round.*

Among the many backward glances, to consider his own past and where the later present time in which he writes, one other poem adds a further element of displaced time. In 'The Prophet' he takes an old guide book to the Netherlands, and interprets its phrases in the light of his own hard-earned experience. It is longer than many of Blunden's poems, and for a harsher observer the out-dated pages could have provided an excuse for mockery, but Blunden uses it with gentle humour, and sympathy for the three periods concerned - the original writer, his own war years, and his later observing self. He places all three in the natural elements of the landscape and uses this historical framework to underline the hazards of his own experiences in it.

It is a country,
Says this old guide-book to the Netherlands,
- Written when Waterloo was hardly over,
And justified 'a warmer interest
In English travellers' - Flanders is a country
Which, boasting not 'so many natural beauties'
As others, yet has history enough.
I like the book; it flaunts the polished phrase
Which our forefathers practised equally
To bury admirals or sell beaver hats;
Let me go on, and note you here and there
Words with a difference to the likes of us.
The author 'will not dwell on the temptations
Which many parts of Belgium offer'; he
'Will not insist on the salubrity
Of the air.' I thank you, sir, for those few words.
With which we find ourselves in sympathy.
And here are others: 'here the unrivalled skill
Of British generals, and the British soldier's
Unconquerable valour ...' no, not us.
Proceed.
'The necessary cautions on the road'...
Gas helmets at the alert, no daylight movement?
'But lately much attention has been paid
To the coal mines.' Amen, roars many a fosse
Down south, and slag-heap unto slag-heap calls.
'The Flemish farmers are likewise distinguished
For their attention to manure.' Perchance.
First make your mixen, then about it raise
Your tenements; let the house and sheds and sties
And rich triumphal opening on the mud
Inclose that Mecca in a square. The fields,
Our witness saith, are for the most part small,
And 'leases are unfortunately short.'
In this again perceive veracity;
At Zillebeke the cultivator found
That it was so; and Fritz, who thought to settle
Down by Verbrandenmolen, came with spades,
And dropped his spades, and ran more dead than alive.
Nor, to disclose a secret, do I languish
For lack of a long lease on Pilkem Ridge.

While in these local hints, I cannot wait
But track the author in familiar ground.
He comes to Menin, names the village names
That since rang round the world, leaves Zillebeke,
Crosses a river (so he calls that blood-leat
Bassevillebeek), a hill (a hideous hill),
And reaches Ypres, 'pleasant, well-built town.'
My Belgian Traveller, did no threatening whisper
Sigh to you from the hid profound of fate
Ere you passed thence, and noted 'Poperinghe.
Traffic in serge and hops'? (The words might still
Convey sound fact.) Perhaps some dim hush envoy
Entered your spirit when at Furnes you wrote,
'The air is reckoned unhealthy here for strangers.'
I find your pen, as driven by irony's finger,
Defend the incorrectness of your map
With this: it was not fitting to delay,
Though 'in a few weeks a new treaty of Paris
Would render it useless. Good calm worthy man,
I leave you changing horses, and I wish you
Good blanc at Nieuport. - Truth did not disdain
This sometime seer, crass but Cassandra-like.

Notes & Sources
Martin Taylor, *Overtones of War*, Duckworth, 1996
Desmond Graham, *The Truth of War: Owen, Blunden and Rosenberg*, Carcanet, 1984
Robyn Marsack, *Edmund Blunden, Selected Poems*, Carcanet, 1982

Blunden's grave in Long Melford churchyard.

BIBLIOGRAPHY

Undertones of War, Edmund Blunden, London, Cobden-Sanderson, 1928; Penguin Books, 1984

Poems 1914-30, Edmund Blunden, London, Cobden-Sanderson, 1930

War Poets 1914-1918, Edmund Blunden, London, The British Council/Longmans, 1958 (Writers and their Work series)

Edmund Blunden, Alec M. Hardie, London, The British Council/Longmans, 1958, (Writers and their Work series)

Edmund Blunden. A Biography, Barry Webb, London, Yale University Press, 1990

Edmund Blunden. Selected Poems, ed. Robyn Marsack, Manchester, Carcanet, 1982

Overtones of War, ed. Martin Taylor, London, Geo. Duckworth & Co., 1996

More Than a Brother, ed. C. Z. Rothkopf & Barry Webb, London, Sexton Press, 1996

The Truth of War: Owen, Blunden and Rosenberg, Desmond Graham, Manchester, Carcanet, 1984

In Honour of Edmund Blunden, ed. J. E. Morpurgo, Christ's Hospital, 1997

Siegfried Sassoon, the Making of a War Poet: a Biography 1886-1918, Jean Moorcroft Wilson, London, Geo. Duckworth & Co, 1998

An Anthology of War Poems, compiled by Frederick Brereton, introduction by Edmund Blunden, London, Collins, 1930

The Poems of Wilfred Owen, ed. and intro. Edmund Blunden, London, Chatto & Windus, 1931

Poetry of the Great War, ed. Dominic Hibberd & John Onions, London, Macmillan, 1986

The Great War & Modern Memory, Paul Fussell, Oxford, Oxford University Press, 1975

Heroes' Twilight, Bernard Bergonzi, London, Constable, 1965

Thiepval, Michael Stedman, London, Leo Cooper, 1995

The Cellars of Marcelcave. A Yank Doctor in the BEF, C.J. Gallagher, Shippenburg, Burd Street Press, 1998

Stockport Lads Together. The 6th Cheshire Territorials 1908-1919, David Kelsall, Stockport Metropolitan Borough Council Leisure Services, 1989

A History of The Black Watch (Royal Highlanders) in the Great War 1914-1918, Wauchope, London, The Medici Society, 1926

The History of The South Wales Borderers, 1914-1918, C. T. Atkinson, London, The Medici Society, 1931

157

History of The East Lancashire Regiment in the Great War 1914-1918, Nicholson & MacMullen, Liverpool, Littlebury Bros, 1936

The 18th Division in the Great War, Nichols (Quex), London, Wm. Blackwood & Sons, 1922

The War the Infantry Knew, Captain J. C. Dunn, London, Jane's Publishing Company, 1987

Order of Battle Division Part 3A, Newport, Ray Westlake Military Books,

A Record of the Engagements of the British Armies in France & Flanders 1914-1918, E. A. James, London, London Stamp Exchange 1990

British Regiments 1914-1918, E. A. James, London, Samson Books, 1978

The Cross of Sacrifice, S. D. & D. B. Jarvis, Reading, Roberts Medals, 1993

Official History of The War: Military Operations France & Belgium 1916, vol 2, Edmonds, London, Imperial War Museum, 1992

Official History of The War: Military Operations France & Belgium 1917, vol.2, Edmonds, London, Imperial War Museum, 1992

Official History of The War: Military Operations France & Belgium 1918, vol.1, Edmonds, London, Macmillan & Co., 1935

Commonwealth War Graves Commission records, Maidenhead

W0/95/2582 Public Record Office, Kew

INDEX